ANN PELLEGRENO   1967 ——
AMELIA EARHART   1937 ----

DEANA KIZER

WORLD FLIGHT   THE EARHART TRAIL

WORLD

THE

THE IOWA STATE UNIVERSITY PRESS / AMES

FLIGHT
EARHART TRAIL

ANN HOLTGREN PELLEGRENO

FRONTISPIECE: July 7, 1967, just after landing at Oakland. Left to right, Bill Polhemus, navigator; Lee Koepke, owner of Lockheed; Ann Pellegreno, pilot; Colonel William R. Payne, copilot.

Composed and printed by
The Iowa State University Press

First edition, 1971

International Standard Book Number: 0-8138-1760-9
Library of Congress Catalog Card Number: 70-153161

To the women and men who have accepted
past challenges in aviation and to
those who will accept them in the future

CONTENTS

CONTENTS

PREFACE

PERHAPS IN A LETTER written by Amelia Earhart to her husband George Palmer Putnam before one of her flights lay the beginning of our flight. Without the last flight of Amelia Earhart, our 1967 flight would never have occurred.

> Please know that I am quite aware of the hazards. I want to do it because I want to do it. Women must try to do things men have tried. When they fail, then failure must be but a challenge to others.

Amelia Earhart's final challenge, a global flight in a Lockheed 10, was to be my first. I wanted to complete that thirty-year-old flight plan.

Much gratitude is due my husband Don who said, "Go ahead if you want," and then helped on all phases; my parents Mr. and Mrs. Clifford C. Holtgren for always assisting and encouraging my endeavors; and my sister Lois without whose companionship growing up would have been doubly hard.

I thank Lee Koepke for the hours spent preparing the plane for the flight and keeping it in A-1 condition, Bill Polhemus for devoting time to getting the flight underway and then keeping it "on course," and Bill Payne who shared the flying hours and whose suggestions resulted in my becoming a better pilot. I especially thank their wives—Larraine, Jan, and Jean, and their children for letting "husbands and fathers" partake in this venture.

PREFACE

Without the assistance of the following companies the flight might never have become a reality.

Air Canada
Aircraft and Airport Services
Champion Spark Plug
Collins Radio Corporation
Flite-Tronics
Garwin-Weston
Goodyear Tire and Rubber Company
Jeppesen and Company
King Radio
Kollsman Instrument Corporation
Pan American Airways
Polhemus Associates, Incorporated
Shell Aviation

Appreciation is due also Joe Allendorf and Harry Fisk from Eastman Kodak for assistance and advice regarding cameras and films; Emerson Mehlhose for flying his airplane to Wichita to bring us back from Wichita when we delivered the plane for fuel tank installation; Harvey Gordon for timely assistance in photography; David Marsh for plating the pitot tubes and flying me to pick up the drift meter; John Hancock for assistance in procuring equipment; Martin Oosta from the Willow Run FAA office for his cooperation on necessary aircraft documents; Phil Davies from PAI who was always "on call" during the flight; Betty Hendricks for sewing my wardrobe; Mr. and Mrs. Wight for their "map in the window" during the flight; Bill Hendricks whose instrument flying skills were twice utilized; Frank Osborn, Ken Bunn, Irv Freimark, and Jerry Gordon for assistance when the plane was being prepared for the flight at A & A; and Lewis Belleau, Paul Sibson, and Dorothy and Dwight Reynolds who were the "spark plugs" for "Ann Day" in Saline.

I thank Bess Tefft and the members of the Ann Arbor Writer's Round Table for helpful comments on manuscripts related to the flight, and Merritt Bailey, Director of the Iowa

State University Press, and Marcy Haque, Manuscript Editor, for their suggestions during the preparation of this manuscript.

Additionally, I would like to thank the thousands who wished us well and the hundreds of people, in this country and abroad, who assisted the flight in so many ways.

A.H.P.

PART ONE

THE COMMEMORATIVE FLIGHT

1937-1967

ON THE MORNING OF JULY 2, 1937, Amelia Earhart, flying a twin-engine Lockheed 10 Electra on a round-the-world flight, searched for Howland Island, a tiny flat-top mountain lying in the middle of an endless blue ocean.

The Lockheed had been airborne since midmorning the previous day when the wheels of this gasoline-laden plane rolled dangerously close to the end of the dusty runway at Lae, New Guinea, before leaving the ground. Past the end of the runway, the overweight plane settled oceanward, flying so low that the propellers flung plumes of salt spray behind. Then the Lockheed climbed slowly on course for a lone island some 2600 miles away. Those who had watched the spectacular take off wondered where the flight would end. They knew there was no immediate return for this pilot. She had never turned back from anything in her life!

All day the Lockheed flew above the ocean. Then the sun slipped below the horizon and the silver plane was engulfed in the darkness of the Pacific night.

Red instrument lights in the cockpit must have been comforting in a unique way to the skilled woman pilot who guided this flight as she had so many other record-breaking endeavors. Ahead must come either the refuge of one small island or nothing. The Lockheed cruised steadily toward the mid-Pacific, an area where no doldrums separate the tradewinds of the southern and northern hemispheres and where towering thunderheads brew eternally above an ocean peaceful by name.

Near the middle of the night Lieutenant Blakeslee of the Ontario, a coal-burning beacon ship from Samoa on station midway between Lae and Howland, noted that a frontal system had moved in. The overcast and rain persisted until near dawn.

Commander Thompson of the Coast Guard cutter Itasca, moored offshore Howland since June 23, had done all in his power to insure that Amelia Earhart locate the island and land safely. The ship, however, was in contact with about half a dozen stations and utilized frequencies ranging from 200 to 16,960 kilocycles. Under these conditions, communications, time zones, frequencies, and instructions could amass to the point of overwhelming complexity. Nevertheless, the radio equipment on the Itasca had been calibrated for the two frequencies—3105 (day) and 6201 (night)—on which Earhart would be transmitting and receiving.

At 2:45 a.m. Howland Island time, men in the radio room of the Itasca heard a fragmentary message from Earhart. "Cloudy and overcast." Though no call sign was heard, one of the men recognized her low flat monotone from monitoring previous flights. Silently, they waited for another message.

Had those words implied that her navigator Fred Noonan was unable to shoot the stars for an accurate fix? Finding a break in the overcast, sighting the proper stars, and obtaining a reading from a hand-held bubble octant in perhaps turbulent air were monumental tasks.

The continuous drone of the two radial engines must have contributed to the growing fatigue of both pilot and navigator. Did Noonan inform Amelia that their fate now depended upon dead reckoning, a process whereby a compass heading is computed using forecast winds? Was this primitive and not always accurate means their only hope? Amelia had used this method when she had flown the Atlantic and Pacific solo, but then she had been flying toward large continental land masses, not a tiny island.

Although other trans-Pacific routes had been considered, going via Howland Island had been chosen as politically most expedient. Pan American Airways was using Wake Island as a base for seaplanes but the construction of a runway there, in light of the proximity of the Japanese mandated islands and other disputed Pacific Island groups, might easily have aroused suspicions of a potential military threat by the United States.

At 3:45 a.m. on that fateful July 2, the men in the radio room of the Itasca heard Amelia say that it was overcast and that she would listen on 3105 kilocycles. Although a reply was sent from the ship, apparently Amelia never heard it. A few minutes later she called again and a barely distinguishable "partly cloudy" came into the radio room.

The Itasca continued sending homing signals and weather on the prearranged schedule. Several other transmissions were received from Earhart, but only once did she reply directly to a query from the ship. At 8:44 a.m. the last transmission picked up by the Itasca was heard. "We are on the line of position 157-337. Will repeat this message. We will repeat this message on 6201 kilocycles. Wait. Listening on 6201. We are running north and south."

This transmission was by voice on 3105 kilocycles with a signal strength of S-5, the highest volume. Nothing was heard on 6201 kilocycles. Earhart was asked to remain on 3105. No other message was received from the plane.

Commander Thompson noted that weather in the Howland Island area was clear. However, forty miles to the northwest a black wall of clouds hovered.

One can imagine Amelia Earhart and Fred Noonan straining to see one small point of land, working frantically at radio knobs, listening for transmissions which never came, and throughout, realizing fuel was running low. Noonan was probably shooting the sun, trying to determine the position of the Electra. But what was his reference for the 157-337 line of position. Without a cross sighting, he could only guess. The Electra flew on, a living legend at the controls.

. . .

This was my understanding of the Earhart incident as, thirty years later, my crew and I peered intently through the windows of another Lockheed 10 Electra, sistership to Earhart's. After having flown three-quarters of the way around the world, we had deliberately placed ourselves in the Howland Island area as nearly as possible to the same time of year and day. My navigator was using the same technique Noonan had, shooting a sun line of position with the sextant. Even with our superior equipment, we as yet had not located the strategic island.

Exhausted from having left Lae, New Guinea, at 6:00 a.m. the day before, flying all day and all night with only a fuel stop at Nauru Island, we now saw nothing but scattered rainstorms. The splashing raindrops beneath them looked to me like waves unfurling repeatedly yet to no avail against a distant sandy beach. Between the rainsqualls streaks of sunlight glinted against the sea. Circling at 1000 feet, we looked for the island, mistaking as that other crew might have done, every cloud shadow for that speck of land.

"We have enough fuel for another twenty minutes of searching," my navigator informed me over the interphone. "Then we'll have to go on."

Since there was no longer a runway on Howland, our "safe harbor" was Canton Island, 421 miles southeast.

Not locate Howland? It was unthinkable after the months of preparation and the dream of completing the 1937 flight plan. We had to find Howland Island. We had come too far to give up now!

THE BEGINNING

THE PARALLELS IN AMELIA EARHART'S LIFE and mine are shared perhaps with all girls who dare to be as they wish and do as they want. Amelia and her younger sister Muriel never lacked adventure, whether factual or fanciful. No doubt they enjoyed wearing the gymsuits their mother made, which gave them unprecedented—and in the eyes of some, outrageous—freedom in that era when hoop rolling was still considered the proper ladylike exercise. Mrs. Earhart simply ignored the raised eyebrows of the neighbors.

Searching for thrills far greater than hoop rolling could afford, the two girls once constructed a roller coaster. The upper end of the track was attached to the garage roof. Even though the track collapsed on the first run and sent cart and Amelia tumbling, she said, "It's just like flying!"

My younger sister Lois and I collaborated in many ventures, some of which can never be confessed on a printed page. And of course we preferred to tackle our projects in blue jeans rather than in anything resembling a skirt. Just how could we wear skirts and build tree houses in the large cottonwood trees, chase a solidly hit baseball, kick a football, or throw a basketball through a hoop?

Lois and I constructed "sailing platforms" by nailing several boards on a wooden frame and attaching roller skate wheels underneath. When March winds whipped through our suburb south of Chicago, we flew down the street, balancing on the skittish platform, each gripping two corners of a billowing canvas used as a sail. Occasionally, we peered around the edge of our sail for oncoming cars. Although we were bruised from tumbling, the sense of reckless freedom more than compensated. How tousled our hair became, but how great was our satisfaction in catching a free flight with the wind.

One day we decided to climb to the top of our house roof. Tennis shoes gripped red shingles as we scrambled upward. Finally, the peak, and from there—the tops of trees, the roofs of houses, the gray-yellow prairie stretching southward. We waved to a slightly horrified neighbor, who, we later learned, had called Mother to warn her of the impending disaster. Using good sense, Mother didn't even come outside. Had we encountered any difficulty descending from that steep roof, we never would have admitted it or hollered for assistance because Dad always said, "Climb anything you want, but don't expect me to get you down!" Not only did we have an abundance of schemes, but once undertaken, they were always carried out to their sometimes unpredictable conclusions.

The same general attitude prevailed when we constructed a sled from barrel stays and then insisted Dad pull us behind the car on snow-covered unimproved roads. Such speed! Such risk and exhilaration as the runnerless sled swerved from side to side, sometimes leaving the ground as it bumped over ruts.

Or, when we fashioned ski-bindings from tin cans and doorsprings, attached them to our four-foot skis, and challenged the steepest hill near grandmother's farm in Michigan.

Or, when my sister, my cousins, and I decided to build a bridge across the river on the farm. Using ax and crosscut saw, we felled two trees, dragged them into place using ropes and levers, and anchored the two stout beams to the river-banks. A puncheon flooring and a handrail were lashed on the twenty-foot span. For ten year's the bridge remained and then my uncle hauled it out with a tractor. During those years it had sagged slightly, but to us it remained a supreme feat.

Amazingly, none of us received broken bones although we swung across the river on ropes, rode calves, crawled almost to the tips of the willow branches which leaned lazily across the creek behind the barn, or cantered the huge Belgians down the lane—bareback. Life at home seemed tame after a visit to the farm.

Ever since Dad had taught me to read using the Chicago Tribune funnies, I eagerly anticipated the books and magazines which came to the house. Devouring them, I experienced much the same exhilaration and satisfaction that I felt during my more daring escapades. Often I burned a flashlight under the bedcovers to finish a novel, biography, adventure story, or book on the outdoors. When nothing else was available, I read encyclopedias, taking a giant tome on my lap and leafing through it until something of interest was found.

Many times I went my own way, an individualist of sorts, simply because that was the way I wanted to go and apparently no one wished to venture in the same direction.

The year I was thirteen, a neighbor who owned a filling station offered me a job pumping gas, fixing flats, and pouring oil into those intriguing engines. Seeing nothing wrong with this arrangement, I was willing to cut my hair to look more like a regular employee.

"Besides," the owner said, "I'd rather employ Ann than lots of boys."

My parents objected, saying that a gas station was no place for a girl. I was sure I would be an asset to the business and the job offered far more promise and excitement than the ones girls were usually given as well as the chance perhaps to work on engines. Amelia too had wanted to work on engines and she had considered opening a shop where girls could tinker with all sorts of machinery. When I applied for auto shop during my senior year of high school, my advisor thrust me firmly back into the academic classroom.

Airplanes had always been remote objects, flying overhead on their way to Midway Airport, and coming into sharper focus only when I was taken there to meet relatives. A shiver would run through me as I watched the giants of the night taxi toward the terminal, red and green lights glowing. At that time the planes seemed like voyagers from an unknown realm, so foreign to me was the world aloft.

Watching planes depart was worse. I waited until appropriate good-byes had been said, then hurried to the observation deck and ran outside. Starters whined, propellers turned slowly, and then black exhaust curled out as the round engines coughed and finally caught with a steady roar. The plane trundled slowly to the runway, waited what seemed an interminable interval, and then, engines snarling, charged forward and climbed toward a distant blue. No matter how far I leaned over the observation-deck railing, trying to keep that plane in sight, silver wings became a silver speck and disappeared. Someday, I had vowed, I would be the one departing, but had never imagined learning to fly.

A year after my husband Don and I graduated from the University of Michigan, we became interested in flying. On August 29, 1960, my first ride in an airplane and first flight lesson occurred simultaneously. The weather was not conducive to an introductory flight lesson—low scud clouds scurried under a gray overcast. As the little blue Aeronca Champ bumped along the sod runway gathering speed for take off, I was happy. At last I was going aloft in a "flying machine." All I wanted to do was gaze at the land below and enjoy the wonder of flight. My instructor had other ideas. He wanted to teach me turns. The fabric-covered plane bounced in the air currents like a small boat on rough water. Each time I tried to circle the plane, we lost altitude. Finally, several attempts later, the instructor took over and headed toward the airport. Soon, as if we were on a gigantic slide, the plane descended and touched smoothly.

Slightly dizzy from the bumping and turning, I nevertheless knew I would learn to fly and make that airplane do exactly as I wished. Arriving home, I realized I had driven through a red light and stop signs. Though my head still buzzed from the noise of the airplane engine, I knew the next flight would not find me simply entranced—I would also be determined to learn to fly.

Earhart wrote about her first solo. "I felt silly. I hadn't done anything special. My first solo had come and gone without anything to mark it but an exceptionally poor landing." ("The Fun of It")

I felt different about my first solo. When the little blue plane and I went aloft together, I felt as if a kindred spirit of the sky realm had been released finally from earth. I was scared, but at the same time exhilarated. Breathing came with difficulty and I forced my somewhat petrified muscles to obey my commands. Still, I enjoyed the red and gold patterns of a Michigan autumn and watched the sky turn deep violet as the sun slipped below the horizon.

After bouncing a little on my first landing, I recovered by adding power. Then I taxied back quickly for another circuit. This time dusk came rapidly, shrouding the airport. As if someone above were taking care of me, I turned on final, cut the power, and glided earthward. Wheels touched the turf as softly as leaves fall on still water, and the plane and I were engulfed in the velvet of the coming night.

During the summer of 1961 Don and I purchased a small two-place airplane. Had we not bought a plane, we might not have met the person who held the key to the round-the-world flight. That person was Lee Koepke, airline mechanic, who gave our plane its required annual inspection.

One April evening in 1962, Lee was working on our plane. The sun was sliding behind masses of towering cumulous clouds massed on the western horizon—an approaching storm. I was sitting on the bench outside the small white building which served as airport office and gathering place for air-minded people. Lee sat beside me.

"Do you know what I'm rebuilding?" he asked.

"No," I replied. With Lee it had to be an airplane. The real question was what type.

"A Lockheed 10. A sistership to the one Amelia Earhart flew around the world."

"Oh," I said, and waited for him to continue. What did a Lockheed 10 look like?

"The thirtieth anniversary of her last flight is coming up in a few years," Lee said. "You know, the one where she got most of the way around the world and then disappeared somewhere in the Pacific."

He sat quietly a moment, and then went on. "I think she made the flight in 1936. Maybe it was 1937. I'll have to check."

"I don't know either," I admitted.

"Well, I was thinking," Lee paused several seconds and then grinned, his blue eyes fixed on mine, "that you might fly it around the world—sort of commemorate that other flight."

"Me fly around the world? Why, Lee, that would be ridiculous in any plane! I have only a hundred hours flying time, mostly in Michigan."

"We can think about it. After all, I've got a lot of rebuilding to do and with several years to go, maybe you'll have more flying time."

"Oh, Lee, really, we could never do anything like that." I began to chuckle.

He looked at me quizzically. I shrugged my shoulders and said, "Maybe someday."

What an impossible idea, I thought, and yet the challenge was there, tempting and perhaps nagging at my subconscious. I knew very little about the Earhart flight, only that she had attempted it after she had flown across the Atlantic solo and set some other records. I had done none of those things and the farthest I had flown was from Ann Arbor, Michigan, to Rockford, Illinois.

As my husband Don and I drove home that evening, I told him about Lee's suggestion.

"You know how it is with those projects," Don said. "It may take him ten years to rebuild that airplane. Maybe he'll never get it done!"

THE LOCKHEED 10A

MEN HAVE REBUILT WACOS, Stearmans, and Piper Cubs, but I found it hard to imagine someone rebuilding a thirty-year old twin-engine plane with a fifty-five-foot wingspan. The plane was Lee's Lockheed, a silver phoenix which rose from a wrecked and battered aluminum hulk and soared skyward.

The Lockheed 10A was certainly not designed for a world flight since it carried only 250 gallons of fuel in the wing tanks, nor was it a plane for a luxury flight today. Yet, Lee had a dream of having this sistership, virtually the same as Amelia Earhart's, flown around the world to complete her flight plan.

The Lockheed Electra Lee eventually rebuilt (serial 1112) originally carried the Canadian registration of CF-TCA and was delivered to Trans-Canada Air Lines on October 6, 1937. For the next ten years it was transferred from Trans-Canada to the RCAF and back at least four times, spending some sixty months with the airline and fifty-six months with the military, carrying the registration of 1526.

In 1946 the Electra was sold as surplus by the Canadian War Assets as CF-BTD and was purchased by the Thunder Bay Flying Club in Fort William, Ontario, where it remained until February 1947. Then, with the same registration, it was sold to W. C. Siple of Dorval, Quebec, who kept it until August when H. C. Moody of Decatur, Illinois, bought it and registered it as N79237. In April 1950 it joined five other Electras owned by Wisconsin Central Airways, Inc. and was based at Truax Field, Madison, Wisconsin. Lee, working as a mechanic for the airline, helped maintain the planes.

A year later, increased passenger loads forced the purchase of DC-3's and the Lockheeds were sold. N79237 went to the Mid Sky Company at Northbrook, Illinois. Named Lady Alice, the Lockheed carried still another registration, N1285. Sometime during these years, blue Plexiglas was installed in the fuselage windows and the plane was seen frequently in the Great Lakes area. Then Midway Airlines which operated the airport shuttle between Meigs, Midway, O'Hare, and Sky Harbor acquired the Lockheed. In 1957 Bankers Life and Casualty bought the plane and in August 1959 sold it to International Air Services. Any semblance of paint was removed and the Electra emerged with a highly polished aluminum skin.

Lee was transferred to Detroit and rented a house just across the road from Willow Run Airport. In the fall of 1959 Great Lakes Airmotive, located less than a quarter of a mile from his house, bought the plane. Lee and other mechanics inspected the entire plane and replaced ribs and skin in the tail section where corrosion was found. In the logbooks was the notation that the right wing and gear had been replaced after the plane groundlooped in 1952.

In the fall of 1960, Lee was again called to work on the Lockheed. A pilot who had been checking carburetor heat on take off pulled the wrong lever and the gear came up too soon.

However, luck was not with N79237, or maybe it should be said that fate was on Lee's side, because in December 1961, another accident occurred. Airborne, the pilot tried to retract the wheels. The gear box, loosened by a hard landing previously, tore loose and bent the torque tube. The gear would not function and the plane belly landed on a snow-covered runway.

After this incident, Great Lakes Airmotive decided to sell the plane and Lee approached them about buying it. But the price was too high. The Lockheed was sold, but not to Lee. The purchaser asked Lee to help strip the Electra of engines, radio gear, and instruments. Since the new owner could not take the fuselage and wings with him, they were scheduled to be destroyed during an airport fire department drill. Lee, however, intervened. After installing a temporary strut on the right gear and removing the wings, he towed the plane to his quonset hut, several hundred feet from his home. The back wall of the quonset was removed to get the fuselage and wings inside. Then the fuselage was hoisted on a dolly to hold the weight off the gear.

The tedious reconstruction began. The two engines were among the most expensive items. To procure the parts required for them, Lee purchased four engines—a run-out (needing complete overhaul) and three from damaged aircraft. One crankshaft was sent to Texas for modification and another to the manufacturer for rebuilding. The bill for the latter was $600!

The man who had purchased the Electra from Great Lakes Airmotive was willing to sell the two damaged Hamilton Standard propellers and from these Lee salvaged one. A converted BT-13 propeller provided the other.

Lee's biggest problems were repairing the landing gear and the cracked right wing spar. He found drawings of repairs which had been made on the spar previously and Lockheed Aircraft sent others, but none were of the particular area needed. Using the points of the available drawings, Lee drew a blueprint for the repair of the top spar cap and submitted it to the Federal Aviation Administration for approval. The bottom spar repair was a duplication of another repair made by Wisconsin Central. In fact, some of the old repair was redone!

Lee contacted Lockheed Aircraft for the drawing of the gear pivot casting which would have to be made by a specialty shop. Fortunately, he obtained a quotation for having a mold made and casting poured. However, the part had to be milled and the shop owner told Lee, "If you need another one, it'll cost double."

The aluminum skin on the lower side of the wing inboard of the right gear had been torn when the gear retracting mechanism had broken and Lee replaced the damaged metal.

Instruments from the "Bamboo Bomber" which Lee had hoped to rebuild were sent to an instrument shop for overhaul and gyro instruments for the copilot's side of the Lockheed were purchased.

By July 1966 the plane was ready for assembly. Wings and fuselage were taken to a hangar at Willow Run. Soon the silver bird was awaiting its first flight. A pilot friend of Lee's sat in the left seat and Lee in the right. Later Lee admitted, "I suppose I was smiling like a Cheshire cat when that plane left the ground."

In October, a pilot I knew walked into the aviation establishment where I worked as a flight instructor. He leaned on the counter and said, "I was flying with Lee in his Lockheed yesterday."

"About noon?" I asked.

He nodded.

"Does it look like a D-18?"

Another nod.

"Then I saw it yesterday when I was over there working on landings and take offs with a student. I do remember a Lockheed calling for take-off permission from the tower."

"That's right. We flew around for about an hour."

"I didn't know that was Lee's plane. Just didn't register. Anyway, I was busy with my student. To be truthful I didn't realize Earhart had flown a twin-engine plane around the world. I wouldn't have known what a Lockheed 10 looked like."

"Lee is still talking about a girl to fly his Lockheed around the world."

"He mentioned it to me several years ago, but the thirtieth anniversary was this past summer, wasn't it? Too late now."

"Well," the pilot continued, "my wife thinks that Earhart went down in 1937. Maybe you could check that. By the way, who are you taking as navigator?"

"I didn't say I was going yet. Besides, I haven't seen Lee for over a year."

"That's a big ocean out there, you know. And that plane is thirty years old."

"Really! And now I suppose you're going to tell me it's a far-fetched idea to fly that plane around the world!"

He chuckled.

Early in December I drove to Willow Run Airport to buy some gaskets for an aircraft engine my husband and I were majoring (overhauling). Wind was whipping large white snowflakes around the corner of the Great Lakes hangar. The Lockheed was parked on the north side. As soon as the gaskets were stuffed in my purse, I asked the parts manager if he thought Lee would mind if I took a look inside the plane.

"Probably not," the man replied.

Quietly, I slipped out the side door, and, feeling almost an intruder, walked toward the plane, footsteps muffled by the snow. The canvas engine covers were flapping in the wind and the aluminum skin was a dull gray, matching the sky. The door was ajar.

"Anybody in there?" I hollered. The only reply was the soft whine of the wind. I climbed aboard, walked up the slanting aisle, and sat in the pilot's seat.

Looking out the window at the wing, I thought, "Heavens— this is such a big plane I'll never be able to fly it. And look at all those gauges!" There were so many more than in the smaller twin-engine planes I had flown.

The yoke was cold beneath my knitted gloves, but inside I was warm. Snow continued piling against one corner of the windshield and the plane shook slightly from the wind, the motion almost like that produced by engine vibrations. Were the oil pressure needles quivering, the tachometer needles steady?

Then, I imagined hearing the faint voice of a navigator saying, "Left, heading zero-six-zero." How long I sat there I don't know, but finally, feeling chilled and not trusting my senses, I left the plane reluctantly, closing the door carefully.

For Christmas Don gave me Fred Goerner's book, "The Search for Amelia Earhart." While reading this, I realized that the flight had been attempted in 1937! The summer of 1967 would be the thirtieth anniversary of the ill-fated flight. The flight should be completed in a sistership.

A couple of days later when I thought about the book, I knew I wanted to fly a Lockheed 10 on the same route, completing the 1937 flight plan.

"Well, why don't you talk to Lee," Don suggested, reading my thoughts. "See if he was serious."

"I might see what he has to say," I replied, trying to sound calm while my mind was racing. "Maybe I'll drive over there now."

The roads were snow covered, their whiteness made even brighter by the full moon. The sky was black velvet, broken by pinpoints of stars which, shining from their vast distances, seemed no more unattainable than our contemplated goal: a flight around the world.

Lee, his wife Larraine, and I sat at the dining room table. "Remember what you mentioned that time you were working on our plane?" I inquired.

Lee grinned. "That's what I thought you were going to ask." He looked thoughtful a moment and then said, "I still think we could do it and I'll help all I can. We should get busy immediately to obtain financial backing and equipment."

For an hour Lee and I talked. Larraine sat quietly, occasionally adding to the conversation. She didn't appear elated about the idea, but as Lee remarked, "She knew I was kind of crazy when she married me." However, she had no objection to Lee's going on the flight.

We set the take-off date from Oakland, California eastbound for May 20— the date Earhart had left Oakland in 1937. That gave us barely five months—not very much time. Lee said he wanted the plane to go even if he could not.

"It's great of you to say that, Lee," I told him, "but I know you really want to be aboard and I hope it works out."

"I'll keep the plane grounded until the flight," he said. "That way nothing will happen to it."

"Yes, it would be a shame to have everything set and then—no airplane. I think clearances might give us some trouble. In fact, I'm considering flying to Washington this coming Sunday to see about them."

"I'm flying to California the same day for mechanic's school on new airline equipment. Be there a month. I could visit Lockheed and see if they would be willing to help."

"That might be a good idea. Do you think we should tell anyone about our plans?"

"For now, since we may not be able to work out the

problems, maybe we should tell only those who need to know."

"That seems best. You know, I never really thought we would even consider this idea seriously. In fact, I was completely surprised when I realized your plane was flying."

Back home I told Don that Lee was agreeable.

"You know what I told you about this project," Don said. "It's your project. Do it if you want. I'll help only if you really need it."

"That's fine with me. I've been considering flying to Washington, D.C. this Sunday to get started on clearances."

"This coming weekend! Well, I suppose you should. No telling how long it will take to get the flight organized."

Two days were spent in Washington, but the trip yielded only one accomplishment—the procurement of an agreement that the Airplane Owners and Pilots Association would handle flight clearances. Cables would be sent to each country on the itinerary giving expected dates of arrival and departure, and we would be billed later.

The interview with an editor of a monthly magazine to discuss the possibilities of his sponsoring the flight or buying an article concluded with this remark, "Of course, we worked closely with Amelia Earhart and undoubtedly would have purchased her story had she returned. But I'm afraid that unless you were collecting butterflies or making maps we couldn't contribute toward anything like your flight."

Why hadn't I collected butterflies instead of building sailing platforms!

"But," the editor continued, "I'll give you our requirements for submitting articles and photographs. If the flight does go and you decide to write an article, you'll have our format."

At least the door had not been closed completely, but the results of this interview were less than encouraging. A week ago a public relations man had told me the accomplishment of anything these days—especially a project of our scope—rested on secure backing.

Shortly after I returned to Michigan, Lee called from California. He had located a man who rented fuel tanks for aircraft being ferried across the oceans. The tanks came in three sizes. I noted the dimensions and told Lee I would measure the fuselage area in front of the main spar to see which tanks would fit there. The man, however, was not sure he would rent the tanks to us for a month!

In February I flew to New York.

At the offices of a national weekly magazine the editor shook his head. "We have two other world flights we're doing articles on. I can't tell you what they are, but we feel they are far more interesting than your flight.* But you can take my card and if you do write an article perhaps we could look at it. However, I feel your flight wouldn't be of sufficient interest to the general public."

An interview with an advertising firm which handled an Amelia Earhart product was equally discouraging. They were not interested in helping.

The only encouraging encounter was with Al Lewis, editor of "Air Progress," who had purchased several articles from me. He was intrigued with the idea of completing the 1937 flight plan and said he would do everything he could to help. In fact, he wanted an article about the flight—immediately. Someone had enough confidence to buy an article before the venture! He also wanted another article when the flight was completed.

Letters were written to fuel and oil companies, equipment companies, and to anyone we thought might have an interest in assisting the flight. I talked with people on the telephone and in person. The results were not encouraging. Perhaps obtaining financial backing would be more of a problem than anticipated. But I still thought that somehow the flight would go.

Lee visited Lockheed Aircraft Company. Not only did he receive no offer of assistance, but those who listened to his idea even tried to discourage him. However, he did talk with some of the men who had helped Earhart prepare her plane.

On March 6, 1967 the first article on our flight appeared in a Detroit newspaper. Until then we had avoided interviews. The people attempting to help us, however, finally persuaded us

*I already knew what they were. To date neither has been completed.

that a public announcement of the flight might work to our advantage. The subsequent events proved them correct.

On March 9 Lee called. "Someone told me we should call Bill Polhemus. He's president of a navigation research engineering firm in Ann Arbor. Perhaps he might help on the navigation and communication equipment. Why don't you call him?"

I did. A cheerful baritone voice answered the phone.

"Polhemus Associates. Bill Polhemus speaking."

"This is Ann Pellegreno. You don't know me, but someone suggested I call you."

Taking a deep breath, I said, "I understand you know a great deal about navigation equipment and celestial navigation."

"Yes."

"Could you help select equipment for a round-the-world flight?"

"Probably."

"Could you teach someone celestial navigation in a week or two of hard work?"

"That someone is you?"

"Well, more or less at the moment."

After a long pause, Bill said, "Why don't you come to my office at nine tomorrow morning."

FLIGHT PLAN

"LET'S TALK IN MY OFFICE," suggested Bill with a boyish grin as he ushered Lee and me inside.

The pleasant baritone was the same I had heard over the telephone yesterday, but added to this were startlingly blue eyes. Here was a man who wasted little time. Sitting behind his desk, however, he leaned back and looked as if he could listen all day. "Now," he said, "tell me about the flight, what you've accomplished, and what you want to do."

Lee and I told him about the unsuccessful efforts to secure financial backing, about not knowing exactly what equipment was needed, and about our uncertainty as to what was involved in a world flight.

Then Bill said, "Let me call several people and see what I can do about getting your navigation and communication gear, and, perhaps some backing."

Lee and I just looked at each other. Someone was interested, really interested in the flight—someone whose help might make the flight a definite possibility!

Soon Bill was talking with Dr. Gene Marner at Collins Radio Corporation in Cedar Rapids, Iowa. Phrases like "618-T3" and "single sideband" entered the conversation.

What was a 618-T3? Why was this particular transceiver the best for the flight?

Bill listened a few moments, frowned slightly, and said, "No, this is a grass-roots operation. They don't have backing yet."

Occasionally he paused to ask Lee and me more about the flight. How long would we need the transceiver? When were we planning to leave?

When Bill hung up, he told us, "I think Collins Radio will loan you one of their single sideband transceivers. Airlines and the military use them. Collins is interested in helping that way but the transaction has to be cleared through the proper channels. Later today we'll draft a letter describing the objectives of the flight."

Then Bill called the Kollsman Instrument Corporation, talked at some length, and requested the loan of two periscopic sextants.

"Two sextants?" I asked.

"You'll want a spare, especially over the oceans!"

Next Bill called the chief navigator at Air Canada, a personal friend of his, and requested the loan of a Loran set which would enable us to find our position fairly accurately in certain areas of the world.

Lee and I listened as Bill made call after call, admiring his logical yet enthusiastic manner of presenting our flight. Hearing him talk even increased our own confidence in it!

Bill wanted to see a manual on the Lockheed 10, so at noon Lee hurried to Willow Run to get one. That afternoon work on our project continued. Occasionally, Bill took calls related to his business or talked with his employees, but mostly he concentrated on our problems. Outlines were made of what would be needed in terms of equipment and support. Papers accumulated, filled with such items as Loran, GLC and GNC navigation charts, survival gear, and estimated costs for the flight.

Another list noted what should be included in the letters written to the companies which were considering loaning us equipment. I promised to have my letter at Bill's office the next morning. Bill would also write a letter. The two letters and a copy of the news release which had appeared in the Detroit Free Press would be sent to the companies as soon as possible.

When Lee and I left Polhemus Associates at five o'clock,

we felt more progress had been made in this one day than in the previous two months.

Soon we knew definitely that Collins Radio would loan us the 618-T3 transceiver, Kollsman the two sextants, and Air Canada the Loran set. Then Lee reported that the Collins radio required a 24-28 volt system and the Lockheed had a 12-volt system. When he was rebuilding the plane, he could have converted to the higher voltage by having the motors for the gear and flaps rewound. Having already passed that stage however, he now sounded completely discouraged as he reported, "Unless I can find a way to double the voltage, we can't use the Collins. However, there is a firm that might be interested in making up a solid state converter—if there's time."

Transmission on the Collins required more power than the Lockheed's VHF transceivers needed and Lee was worried about burning out one or both of the two 50-amp generators from any lengthy use at near maximum output. With electric gear and flaps this would present problems.

An article about the flight appeared in the Detroit News. Soon afterward Jim Kane, a reporter from the Ann Arbor News, scheduled an interview with us on March 14. That day Lee was washing the plane. Salt spray thrown up by passing cars and blown by westerly winds while the Lockheed had been parked near the airport fence had started corrosive action on the aluminum. Unless the washing and subsequent etching halted the corrosion, the underside of the wings where the damage was the worst would have to be painted.

When Jim arrived, Lee was still washing the plane, so I answered the questions. Later Lee came in and said, "The Lockheed is by the next hangar. If you want pictures, we can walk over."

Approaching the plane, Jim looked dubious. Perhaps he was noting the dented aluminum near the tail, the lack of a snappy paint job, and the tailwheel in today's world of tricycle gear.

After Jim had taken some pictures, Lee asked if we would like to accompany him when he taxied the plane to the southwest ramp where he was keeping it. We accepred. There was no speaker for the radios, so Lee and I wore headsets. After receiving clearance to taxi, Lee gunned the left engine momentarily to swing the plane around to the right. Then the Lockheed moved slowly toward Lee's red truck a half mile distant, the wheels bumped along the taxi strip, the balloon air wheels setting up a steady rhythmic jouncing. When the plane was in position on the ramp and the propellers had stopped, Jim surprised us by saying, "I'd like to go with you on the flight."

Of course the plane would have been over gross, and his accompanying us was an impossibility, but it was good to know that someone else believed in the old plane.

Lee and I still had mixed feelings about the publicity. We realized that our original plan to keep the flight under wraps until it was a sure thing had gotten us nowhere. Our decision to follow the advice of others and let more people know, on the other hand, had won us assistance and encouragement. In spite of the support for the flight which the publicity had gained us, we still saw it, however, as a potential source of embarrassment if our venture failed to materialize. At any rate, we were already committed and would do everything possible to insure completion of the flight plan. No one would ever be able to say we had not tried.

Many hours were spent figuring ways to finance the flight. One stamp collector suggested carrying flight covers. A dealer was found who would be interested in arranging for the covers, advertising them, and taking over the intricacies of corresponding with countries for cancellation information. Amelia Earhart had carried ten thousand covers which had been sold in advance by Macy's for $2.50 each. Cancellations were to have occurred at San Francisco, Karachi, and Honolulu. Her cover had been a single envelope and the three stamps and cancellations would have appeared on it. Because of postal complications today, we were advised to have a cover for each place a cancellation would occur. Upon return to the United States, the covers were to be sold in sets.

FLIGHT PLAN

Set Number 1	Set Number 2	Set Number 3
San Francisco	San Francisco	San Francisco
Natal, Brazil	Karachi	Dakar
Dakar, Senegal	Lae	Singapore
Karachi, Pakistan		Lae
Lae, New Guinea		

Although more than one hundred letters had been written to individuals and companies, only a few had produced positive replies. Therefore, when the phone rang one afternoon, I was pleasantly surprised to hear that Champion Spark Plug was interested in helping. Tony Mougey, its public relations man, outlined the proposal. "We're willing to give you iridium spark plugs, an all-weather ignition harness, exhaust gas temperature gauges, assistance with customs and press conferences, and also a check for $1000 without further delay."

Up to now, nothing like this had occurred. I really did not know how to respond. Was this a fair amount in return for the advertising after the flight? Lee would have to be consulted on the equipment offered. The $1000 was unbelievable and certainly the assistance was needed.

Friday, March 17, Lee, Bill, and I met. The offer from Champion was accepted. Then Bill had some bad news. "I've been flight planning some of the longer legs. After talking with the Lockheed people, I think you're in trouble on the long legs, considering the speeds and fuel estimates in the manual."

I remembered the letter I had received from Lockheed—the Lockheed 10 was not designed for long distances and we were, perhaps, taking an unnecessary risk even attempting the world flight.

"You're in real trouble with weight and range," Bill continued. "I've replotted the leg from Brazil to Africa with a stop at Ascension Island. On the flight from Kwajalein Island to Honolulu, I'd like to see you stop at Johnston Island. I'm really doubtful about the leg from Hawaii to California."

Lee and I listened, feeling the flight less a possibility than ever. If we couldn't get across the Atlantic nonstop, how were we going to fly from Hawaii to California? Go back the way we had come?

"We'll consider anything you suggest," I told Polhemus.

Then it was Lee's turn. He suggested putting two 100-gallon fuselage tanks in front of the main spar and one tank holding 400 gallons behind the main spar. That would give 850 gallons total fuel weighing 5100 pounds. With the weight of the tanks themselves and the additional navigation and communication equipment the plane would be almost 3000 pounds overweight.

The Lockheed's take-off weight for the longer legs was estimated at 13,500 pounds. Earhart's plane had been certified for overgross operations at 16,500 pounds, but she had 550 horsepower engines rated at 600 horsepower at 2250 rpm for take off. Her propellers were two-position—take off and cruise. Our engines were 450 horsepower rated at 450 horsepower at 2300 rpm for take off if a minimum of 87 octane fuel was used. We had the advantage of full-feathering variable-pitch propellers.

Sunday, March 19, Bill and I flight planned. Line after line was drawn on the charts, some straight to the destination, others following radio navigation aids. His maps of the Atlantic equatorial region did not lap correctly, leaving out, for example, the eastern coast of Brazil where Natal was, so Bill figured a triangulation from the two maps and extended a line to Natal's position.

Columns on the blackboard filled with distances, RON's (remaining overnight), estimated times en route, estimated fuel for each leg, and magnetic courses. Alternate routings across the Pacific were drawn. It was hard not to study the maps to observe the territory over which we would fly, but the preliminary plan must be completed. By the time the data on the blackboard had been transferred to paper, and three copies made, the sun had set. But, we now had a more realistic view of the route.

"That must have been some flight in 1937," Bill commented. "Look at those areas in Africa. Nothing but sand. No radio aids either. Not many even now. The more I look at their route and know the equipment they used, the more I respect and admire those two."

I agreed with him.

"Quite a few people have asked what we're calling the flight," I said. "It takes time to explain. Maybe we should have a name for it."

"I don't like the word, 'memorial,' some have used." Bill replied. "Why not call it the Earhart Commemorative Flight."

The name was adopted and those three words conveyed to people what previously had taken three hundred.

Amelia Earhart's Lockheed had been equipped with a three-axis autopilot to relieve the physical strain of flying. My lack of flying experience outside the United States combined with the tight schedule before the flight, the small amount of time I would have in the plane, and no autopilot meant a copilot was mandatory. The first pilot I had asked appeared willing to go when it seemed the flight was not going, but as soon as we made progress, his job became bindingly all important. I began looking for someone else and on a hunch called a pilot I had talked with a couple of times, thinking he might be willing to go on a venture such as this.

"Sure. Why not?" he said. "I'd like to know more about it."

On April 3, Foster Green, who worked for the same airline Lee did, met with Polhemus and me. When he saw the route eastward from Lae, New Guinea, he rubbed his chin thoughtfully.

"We want to duplicate the 1937 flight as nearly as possible," I told Foster. "Even though we can't land on Howland, we'll overfly it providing it can be worked in the routing."

"That's an awful lot of **blue** out there," commented Foster.

"Yes," I agreed. "But look at all those islands."

We laughed. Somehow this remark relieved the tension and talk continued along favorable lines. Finally, Foster said, "I'll go if I can get time off from the airline and my salary from you. After all, I've got a family to feed."

For the previous week, Polhemus had been hinting that our

flight needed him as an overwater navigator. He had been a navigator in the Air Force and had guided the record-smashing B-58 speed run from Washington to Paris in 1961.

I wondered about taking four in the plane. But, as Foster had said, there was a lot of blue out there. Perhaps we did need a navigator. Lee had said he would remain behind if necessary. Lee or Bill, or both? Foster hadn't studied celestial navigation and I had no time to learn the processes. All things considered, Lee and I welcomed Bill aboard. From that time the tempo of the preparations increased considerably.

Navigation to Bill was what music is to some people and flying to others. It was his life. Since retiring from the Air Force, he had not had the opportunity to do as much navigating as he would have liked. Then, too, his business made heavy demands on him. Here was a chance to navigate in rather unusual circumstances. I doubt he could have resisted the challenge even though he knew how much work the flight would entail. He was that kind of person—the bigger the challenge, the more irresistible it seemed to him. Someone had once remarked, "Don't give the job to Polhemus unless you want it finished!"

In January the flight had become almost my full-time job and I had accepted no new flying students. Each day began with a list of things to be accomplished with results reported to Lee and Bill. Had funds been available, a secretary would have been hired.

Unfortunately, most replies to letters requesting assistance were negative, nicely worded, but still **no**. A pleasant surprise was a check for $12.76, the proceeds from a book sale held by the seventh grade at Saline Junior High School where I had taught. That same day, however, our first higher-than-usual telephone bill came—$111.18. I was reluctant to tell Don, as our bills normally were less than twenty dollars. After he saw the amount, we decided the time was now to go for broke, but we had no way of knowing exactly how broke we eventually would be.

EQUIPMENT

★
 ★
★

ON APRIL 9, FOSTER GREEN accompanied me when I took the plane to Wichita, for I had never flown a Lockheed 10. It would remain at Javelin Aircraft for two weeks while fuselage tanks, a fuel dump system, and an oil transfer system were engineered and installed.

Lee, Bill, and I started getting vaccinations, receiving at least two per appointment, sometimes more: typhoid, typhus, tetanus, polio, yellow fever, smallpox.

Two letters requesting assistance brought favorable replies. Jeppeson and Company agreed to supply instrument charts and approach plates. Goodyear Tire and Rubber Company, the only manufacturer of the air wheels needed on the Lockheed, was giving us new tires and tubes. The present ones had been on the plane since before Lee had bought it and were somewhat scuffed and cracked.

At the end of two weeks we had as yet received no call to notify us that the fuel tank installation had been completed. We waited, not too patiently, knowing that each delay of a day meant one day less for equipment installation. The Kollsman sextants and the Loran set arrived.

Cleveland television called as did the Wichita newspapers and the Detroit radio and television stations. New York stations called. As early as 7:00 a.m. and as late as midnight, the phone rang. Now everyone wanted information about the flight. People sent clippings from their local newspapers. Some sent contributions which I acknowledged with a personal thank-you note. A secretary could have been kept busy seven days a week.

In "Last Flight," Earhart wrote, "I want to do a careful account of this final job of getting ready for a long flight. It's really colorful and I think could be made interesting even for non-flyers!" How well she knew the myriad of details involved!

Finally, we were notified that the plane would be ready on Wednesday, May 3. I had to find someone to accompany me on the return flight, as Foster was scheduled with the airline.

Fortunately, a letter from Marvin Kruskopf, an airline pilot who lived near Chicago, had arrived. He had attempted to organize a flight similar to ours but had failed to obtain sufficient financial backing. Since he had offered to help in any way he could, I called him. Not only was he willing to fly back from Wichita with Lee and me, but he would pick us up in his personal airplane at Willow Run the evening before and fly us to Chicago where we would hop a jet to Wichita the following morning.

Tuesday night when Lee arrived from work shortly after midnight, we three jumped into Marvin's plane and soon the lights of the city were behind us.

The steady hum of the engine and the conversation in the front seat lulled me to sleep. Only when the wheels touched the runway did I awaken.

Once aboard the airliner, however, I could scarcely remain calm in anticipation of seeing the Lockheed.

At Wichita we met with a dismal greeting—snow showers, a gray overcast, and a blustery wind. This May 3, 1967 was hardly a spring day. The plane was parked on the ramp as the men finished work on the oil transfer system. What had been empty space inside the plane was now filled with shiny aluminum tanks. The old plane was beginning to look as if a world flight really would be possible. Dave Blanton from Javelin Aircraft had engineered the systems and supervised the installation. He explained filling the tanks, transferring the fuel, and the operation of the oil transfer system. Special limitations had been imposed on the plane in this configuration. One of the many was NO SMOKING! Both never-exceed and cruise speeds had been reduced.

The cost of the installations totaled $3200. Two checks were signed over—the one for $1000 from Champion and the other for $2200 from our personal savings. I agreed with Earhart's idea that futures were to be mortgaged for what one wanted to do!

Then the news media people descended. We were anxious to be on our way but they detained us with the assurance that our delay would be brief. Men from ABC, NBC, and CBS had come. Photographers, cameramen, interviewers, and reporters! A movie camera buzzed near my face. "Just keep talking," a voice instructed.

"How about sitting in the cockpit?" I sat in the cockpit.

"Open the window. Smile. Now put on those headphones. Hold that pose!"

"Let's take some shots of Lee and Marvin. The interviewers want to talk to them," a man hollered.

"Can you open the hatch?" a cameraman yelled.

I didn't relish coming up through the hatch and waving, but the men insisted and Lee opened it.

"OK, when we give the signal, come up through the hatch and wave."

I felt like a jack-in-the-box, but the "act" was repeated three times!

When the newsmen seemed finished it was noon. We had been outside over two hours and I was chilled throughout. Lee, Marvin, and I climbed aboard the plane. Even as we started the engines, cameras clicked and rolled. "Lockheed Two Three Seven," came the voice from the tower over the headphones. "We have a request for you to delay take off until the cameramen have positioned themselves along the runway."

"Roger," I replied.

En route to Cedar Rapids where we had scheduled a meeting with Collins Radio personnel, Lee experimented with the fuel transfer system. Outside, the snow flurries thickened. Inside, we froze, for the heating system had been removed when the tanks had been installed.

The meeting at Collins lasted an hour. The men were

helpful, but they feared their transceiver would not work well in the Lockheed. Lee was now doubly discouraged. For flying around the world we needed an HF (high frequency) set which was capable of transmitting and receiving over longer distances than the line-of-sight VHF (very high frequency) used normally in the States.

To return to Willow Run as quickly as possible, or not wanting to freeze longer than necessary, we climbed to 13,000 feet where 40-knot tailwinds were forecast. Still unthawed from the flight to Cedar Rapids, I knew the only way to get warm again, really warm, was to jump into a steaming bath at home.

Lee, wearing a parka, sat in the single seat aft of the fuel tanks and dozed, his breath generating white vapor. Marvin wrapped a blanket around his feet. I wanted to sit on mine, but that was impossible. The outside air temperature was 4 degrees above zero, but the compensating factor was a groundspeed of nearly 200 mph!

When we opened the fuselage door in front of the Aircraft and Airport Services hangar, the blast of 40-degree air felt like a tropical breeze. Three stiff, cold people watched as the Lockheed was rolled inside the heated hangar where A & A was letting us keep the plane until departure for California.

Lee still worried about the Collins installation. The flight bank account was bankrupt, but our determination had not waned!

On the positive side, the fuel tanks were in, we had new tires and tubes, and the plane was in a warm hangar. Some equipment had arrived. Many people had volunteered to help. Besides, it was too late to even consider turning back.

During the next two days the iridium spark plugs, the ignition harness, and the exhaust gas temperature gauges were installed by "Doc" Anderson from Champion. Engines were checked. Construction was started on an upper instrument panel to accommodate the extra gauges.

Tony Mougey had queried the executive editor of "McCall's" to see if he might want to purchase an article about the flight. The morning of May 9 I received a call from Jim Fixx. A

INTERIOR of fuselage after returning from Wichita. Dump
valve knob is just aft of cockpit on top of right forward fuel tank.
(Courtesy Ann Arbor News)

half-hour discussion followed and a very acceptable offer was
made. An advance would be mailed with the contract, the
balance payable upon receipt of the manuscript.

I called Lee and Bill immediately. What a tremendous
break! What good fortune!

At noon the same day I drove to Willow Run to meet the
camera crew from WXYZ television in Detroit. I had been
invited to appear on their Morning Show May 22 and they

wanted some film of the plane and people involved. Two hours later the "movie" had been shot.

At home was a letter from an insurance broker. During April I had written companies asking for quotations, but when the agencies found that a thirty-year-old plane was to be flown around the world, they balked. That is, all except one—Lloyd's of London, a company I had always associated with the foolish, the unpredictable, the high risk. I smiled. Why, they supposedly would insure anything! Never had I dreamed that company would be called upon to insure a venture in which I was involved.

Lee and I had estimated between $1500 and $2000 for insurance. I tore the letter open. The first figure I saw was the $15,000 at the bottom of the page. Fifteen thousand dollars! Lee and I had originally estimated the cost of the entire flight at that figure. How could such good news and such disheartening news come in a single day! At least there had been six hours of happiness after "McCall's" offer. Somehow the insurance quotation would have to be lowered.

Shortly afterward, an article entitled "Earhart Flight Is GO Despite Insurance Costs" appeared in the Ann Arbor News. A few days later a dollar bill arrived with a note: "Hope the other 14,999 come through!"

So much remained to be done that departure from Oakland was moved ahead to June 1.

Saturday, May 14, I went to the other side of the state to pick up a B-3 drift meter. Having opened almost every carton in the dark warehouse and measured the tube, I found one that was short enough.

By noon I was back at Willow Run where Lee cut a round hole in the top of the fuselage for the sextant mount. The tail of the plane was to be raised to level flight position so Polhemus could sight across the hangar toward a surveyor's transit to align the mount with the centerline of the fuselage. First, a dozen men lifted the tail and a barrel was placed beneath the tailwheel. A jack was inserted, raised, but was not high enough. A taller jack was located. Still not enough. Finally, the nitrogen was let out of the main gear shock struts, lowering the

COCKPIT when interphone, Collins, and additional VHF capability were being installed. Placards beneath instrument panel and above handles read: "For one quart of oil in this engine, turn handle clockwise 58 times."

nose 4 inches. Bill aligned the mount and Lee secured it. This operation should have taken a couple of hours instead of an entire afternoon.

Measurements were made for radio rack materials and the following Monday the aluminum sheet and extrusion were purchased. A mount was ordered for the drift meter. The Collins transceiver, antenna coupler, and mounting racks arrived along with the installation manual. For days afterward the intricate drawings were followed and "miles" of varicolored wires were cut and then connected to the designated terminals as the HF and the intercom were installed.

Flite-Tronics, manufacturer of converters which would jump the 12-volt DC to the 24-volt DC needed for the Collins, was willing to loan four 15-amp converters to the flight. Lee mounted them in parallel to give 60-amps of 24-volt DC.

The bubble light in the sextant, the Loran set, and the drift meter gyro required 110-volt AC current. Lee found an inverter to change the current from 12-volt DC to 110-volt AC.

The hand-operated trailing antenna reel purchased to be used with the Collins and the Loran was too slow and cumbersome, so an electric reel was bought. King Radio gave us an omni head and KR-80 automatic direction finder (ADF) for the nav station and the kit to change the number 2 VHF transceiver from 90 to 360 channels. Someone was always working on the plane. Sundays excepted, Lee was there daily until he left for work at three o'clock. Polhemus Associates had become the flight operations center. Always awaiting us there were letters, telephone calls, and decisions.

Progress was evident, but everything took twice as long, or longer, than anticipated. Departure from Oakland was moved ahead to June 9, and Lee was dubious about having the plane ready even then. Sometimes I became discouraged, but never gave up hope that somehow the flight would occur. Whenever things looked too bad, I called Polhemus. He was always optimistic!

PROGRESS

WHEN FOSTER GREEN HAD BEEN UNABLE to obtain leave from the airline, Bill Polhemus suggested asking Colonel William R. Payne, USAF, a friend of his who had been the pilot on the B-58 speed run. In addition to having flown internationally, Colonel Payne had time in C-45's, a plane similar to the Lockheed 10.

Polhemus's praise of Payne's flying ability, military training, and congeniality, convinced Lee and me that Payne was the man for the job. Bill called Payne and did some verbal arm twisting, I'm sure. A letter requesting a month's leave for Colonel Payne was mailed to the Secretary of the Air Force. It emphasized the part the Air Force had played in past aviation events and that the assistance of Colonel Payne was desired to help make the flight a success.

Two weeks later, on May 20, the leave permission was granted and Payne took over the Washington end of our business, namely working with Kitty Howser of the AOPA on clearances. Most of the clearances received had granted us permission to land, but Indonesia had not replied to repeated cables.

Andre Barroso, an underwriter, helped with the insurance problem. Letters and cables flew between London and Ann Arbor. The Lockheed's vintage was not in our favor and the equipment we carried—most of it on loan and valued in excess of $20,000—had to be insured. Hull coverage for the plane, a special worldwide medical and accident policy, and a million dollars property damage and liability were included. Each time a reply arrived the premium was lower. Our decision to reduce the amount of hull insurance accounted for part of the reduction, but Andy would not stop there. Hoping to bring the quotation lower still, he continued to write letters stressing the safety measures being planned, the equipment aboard, and the crew qualifications. The addition of Colonel Payne also had much to do with the lower rates, I am sure. The quotation came down from $13,000 to $11,000 to $8000, and finally to $4820.

The coverage would extend from Willow Run around the world and back to Willow Run. Don and I had to raise this amount, payable in a lump sum before departure. We had already borrowed $4000, and now even with depleting our savings, we would have to borrow another $2000. This proved difficult. Finally, a bank accepted our collateral and gave us the money, but it had been necessary for the president of the bank to approve a loan for our purpose. During the interview he told me, "I think you're asking for trouble flying that old plane around the world."

When he said that, I couldn't help smiling. Remarks like that never daunted us. Our navigator was the best; our copilot topped by none; the equipment superior! Still, it would be difficult to turn over that check for $4820. Seemingly, that transaction was irrevocable whereas even now we were not one hundred percent sure the flight would go. Don and I decided to wait until almost the last minute to part with the money.

Lee was fortunate to have two steady helpers in John Harden and Phil Neal, both aircraft mechanics. Without their help the plane would not have been as ready as it was. The two remote indicating compasses and two certified altimeters given to us by Garwin-Weston were installed. However, the end of May approached and I wanted more flight time in the plane. Half a dozen take offs and landings were barely sufficient. Now that the cowlings were back in place and work completed on the upper instrument panel, the plane could be flown, even though the fuselage installations were still incomplete.

Bob Smith, a pilot in the Michigan Air National Guard who had time in D-18's, agreed to fly with me. At six o'clock one evening Bob, Lee, Edgar Lesher, and I took off.

Professor of aeronautical engineering at the University of

Michigan, Lesher had offered to take time off from his preparations for record-breaking flights in his experimental airplane to make our performance charts. He would construct tables to designate the take-off distance required at various temperatures, altitudes, and weights. Also he would calibrate the three airspeed indicators—two in the cockpit and one at the navigator's station.

A few miles west of Willow Run, Lesher had a measured course of 3.98 which he used in connection with computations on his experimental airplanes. We descended to 500 feet above the terrain and flew back and forth twice, holding altitude and power settings constant. Lesher timed the flights with a stopwatch and the indications on the three airspeeds were noted. The three indicators would be calibrated in his laboratory, but he agreed to leave them in the plane until after I had done some take offs and landings the next day.

The following morning, Bob Smith's car swung into the parking lot at A & A. An hour later we were at the end of the runway. I locked the tailwheel and eased the throttles forward.

"Go ahead," Bob shouted. "Get that manifold pressure up to 36 inches."

The tail rose. The airspeed needle crept to 50. To 70. Finally when it hovered over 90, I eased back on the yoke and the plane climbed toward the southwest. Lesher had asked us to do a fuel consumption check. At 5000 feet I leveled off, set the manifold pressure to 27 inches, the rpm's to 1850, and switched to the auxiliary fuel tanks. Bob started the stopwatch. Outside air temperature was noted. For a half hour we flew, keeping settings constant. When the time was up, I switched back to the main tanks and turned toward Willow Run.

The first landing was not good. Two small bounces attested that the airspeed had been slightly slow and the tail a little low on touchdown. The next two circuits were better. After the fourth, I felt I was flying the plane more than it was leading me. Happy that the final landing had been good, I taxied to the hangar. When the plane was fueled, I noted to the tenth of a gallon how much each auxiliary tank had taken. Lee removed the airspeed indicators and I took them to Lesher along with the figures from the morning's flight.

Bill Payne arranged for the loan of four units of Air Force fighter pilot survival gear, and on Wednesday, May 31, he scheduled a three-minute stop at Willow Run to deliver them.

Bill Polhemus and I watched as the Saberliner stopped on the ramp. The engines were left running. Colonel Payne, in Air Force blues, carried the canvas bags from the plane. Polhemus introduced us. I offered to show Payne the Lockheed which was visible in the rear corner of the large hangar, but he had no time. In fact, I barely had time to click my Instamatic as he climbed back aboard. A second later the jet moved slowly toward the runway and two minutes later it had disappeared in the northern sky. It had indeed been a three-minute stop!

"Well, what do you think of Payne?" Polhemus asked.

I hardly knew what to say. Make an evaluation after one handshake and a few words? "He seems nice," I told Polhemus. "Very efficient and pleasant."

As Lee and I had trusted Polhemus's judgment before, we did so again. In fact, we credited him with getting the flight "off the ground" so to speak. Now, with some equipment installations incomplete, we were still worried about leaving Willow Run for Oakland on June 7.

Friday evening, June 2, Bill Payne arrived for a weekend of flight briefing and his checkout in the Lockheed. Saturday morning our group met at the airport to test the fuel dump system since we needed an estimate of the time required to dump the 350 gallons allowed from the 450-gallon rear fuselage tanks. The assistant airport manager suggested that the plane be positioned so the tail and dump tube would extend over the grass at the edge of the ramp.

The tail was lifted onto a barrel to more closely simulate level flight attitude, and a slightly smaller barrel with a 35-gallon capacity was placed beneath the end of the aluminum dump tube which extended 2 feet behind the tail cone. Since the fuel would be gushing with considerable force, Lee attached a flexible hose to the tube and put the other end inside the barrel.

The dump valve was opened. Four seconds later the fuel began pouring out. A minute and twenty seconds later the barrel was full. Why, at that rate, it would take more than 10 minutes to dump 350 gallons! Hopefully, we wouldn't have to use the dump system.

Lesher told us his calculations from the speed runs indicated drag was greater than anticipated. That meant at the power settings given in the manual, the plane would not attain the speed it should have. Added antennas, rubber step pads on the wings, fasteners protruding where the de-icing boots had been removed, and the plane's having been damaged several times helped account for this.

When Payne received his checkout in the plane, men were stationed along the first part of the 7500-foot runway so a mark could be placed where the wheels lifted. Lesher, knowing the airport altitude, temperature, take-off weight, and the distance required to become airborne, could project these figures for the over-gross take-off tables.

At noon Tony Mougey and the photographers from Champion arrived to take pictures of plane and crew for advertising purposes. After that the Lockheed was rolled into the hangar where equipment installation continued.

Sunday morning I flew the Lockheed with Payne. Another fuel check was done and then I shot several landings.

During lunch some mysteries of the survival gear were explained, such as the use of the signal mirror and the miniature flare gun. In the event of ditching over water, the raft was to be inflated during the descent so that it would be ready for occupancy upon touchdown. Before the water was hit, the leg straps of the parachute were to be unhooked but the shoulder straps left fastened until contact with the water. Then, after the latter were unhooked, the only thing remaining was to follow the rope to the raft and climb aboard. The six cans of water were to be drunk fairly soon so dehydration would be delayed and the risk of losing them overboard lessened. Payne made the procedures sound reassuringly simple, but in the event of any ditching, land or sea, I wanted to come down close to him. It was that simple!

As I drove him to Detroit Metropolitan Airport for his return flight to Washington, we agreed the outlook was favorable for the proposed Wednesday morning departure if the remaining equipment could be installed. Sunday evening the following comment was entered in my flight journal. "Flew with Bill Payne. Excellent pilot! Great guy! Blue eyes! Nice smile!"

Monday morning, June 5, we were informed that because of the Arab Israeli War, the State Department had banned travel in those and nearby countries—some of them on our route. Payne was contacted and he began planning a route to take us across Africa, but south of the troubled areas.

That afternoon Lee mounted the shiny new Goodyear air wheels. Lesher gave us our performance charts. With the plane at full allowable over-gross weight of 13,700 pounds, and no wind, I was amazed to find the take-off roll was predicted to be almost 6000 feet!

Whenever I arrived at A & A, there was a sheaf of messages: calls from aviation groups, relatives, friends, Chicago television, New York newsmen, Ohio newspapers, UPI, AP. One reporter from Detroit called five times in one day for more facts and to verify information.

Evelyn Kaiser who lived near Riverdale, Illinois, where I had resided until going to college, had done much work in fund raising, writing articles for the newspapers in that area, and general public relations work. I had never met her but she knew my parents and had decided that she would help the flight. Donations had come from Riverdale, from members of the Ann Arbor Zonta Club, from friends, from strangers. My high school, Thornton Township in Harvey, Illinois, and its sister school, Thornridge, had sent nearly a thousand dollars— the result of students' paying a quarter for the privilege of wearing shorts for a day. This money was used for traveler's checks and I don't know what we would have done without it.

Shell Oil Company issued us an international carnet and agreed to grant commercial rates on fuel purchased outside the United States. After all, we had more fuel capacity than a standard DC-3.

At noon on Tuesday Lee said, "We can leave in the morning. I'll work tonight and get as much finished as I can and install the rest en route."

I called Payne at the Pentagon.

But what if we couldn't leave in the morning! By now the news-media people wanted a definite departure time, yet we could not leave until things were right. I told them we planned to depart at 8:00 a.m.

I met Payne's flight at Metro and drove him to Willow Run where he inspected the plane. Lee was adjusting the trailing antenna reel, closing up inspection holes, and making numerous final checks. Work continued on the Collins installation.

My parents, Evelyn Kaiser, Don's parents, and more relatives and friends arrived. After dinner Don and Payne returned to the airport to help Lee. I went home to pack, but the few items barely filled my small suitcase. Extra film was put into a box for storage in a wing locker. More telegrams came and at midnight the phone was still ringing. An hour later Don and Payne arrived with the flight charts they had picked up at Polhemus's office since he had left for London and would join us in Miami.

There was so much to discuss. Payne showed us the medical kit an Air Force doctor had assembled, and manuals detailing emergency procedures for air and sea rescue. My eyes kept closing. The nights without proper sleep, the furious pace of the days, and the continuous pressure to get the flight underway had taken their share of my energy. At three o'clock we decided some sleep was necessary.

And yet, I still had my doubts. Were we really ready? I knew we couldn't turn back. Hundreds of people and many companies had helped us. Polhemus had spent hours on flight preparations, committed his company to assist the flight in any way possible, and accumulated who knows how much in telephone bills. Don and I had about $10,000 invested in the flight and Lee about $500 plus time spent working on the Lockheed. The income so far included about $1500 in donations, the check for $1000 from Champion, payment for the "Air

Progress" article, and an advance payment from "McCall's."

Sleep came slowly. It was unbelievable that in a few hours I would be leaving on a 28,000-mile flight having placed my trust in an old silver Lockheed and the man who had rebuilt her.

WILLOW RUN
OAKLAND
MIAMI

WERE WE REALLY LEAVING this morning? It seemed the same as so many other days except that we had arisen earlier and were at the airport by half-past six.

In the light generated by the huge fluorescents on the hangar ceiling, relatives and friends, not deterred in the least by the damp drizzly weather, inspected the plane and gazed at the gray skies outside. Reporters, television crews, interviewers, and photographers—some from Chicago and Wichita—were there in force. Between talking with them and answering the phone, I loaded my personal gear which included a small box of mementos to be carried around the world for friends. Most of the flight covers were stowed in the nose baggage compartment and the rest in the wing lockers.

When the plane was loaded, the hangar door inched upward, letting the damp moist air inside, and a tractor pulled the plane out. Fuel, the welcome donation of A & A, was poured into the wing and fuselage tanks. Soon afterward, dark clouds streaked past and sheets of rain lashed the airport, sending people scurrying back into the hangar. I shared an umbrella with Jim Kane, the reporter from the Ann Arbor News, who, at this final moment would have needed no encouragement to climb aboard.

As eight o'clock approached, the rain showed signs of stopping. Hurriedly, good-byes were said. As I crawled over the fuselage tanks to the cockpit, someone yelled, "Will you wave from the hatch?"

Though raindrops still spattered on the windshield, I opened the hatch and stood up. Then, Lee secured it and took his seat. We were ready, as ready as we would ever be and still keep our target date with Howland Island. On June 7, 1937, Earhart had flown from Natal, Brazil, to Africa. We hadn't even arrived in California yet!

I gunned the left engine, swinging the plane in a wide arc to keep the propwash away from the people. At the threshold of Runway 14 we heard, "Lockheed Two Three Seven. Cleared for take off." It was 8:10. Facing the southeasterly wind which was bringing the rains, the silver plane charged down the runway, engines thundering, wheels sending geysers behind as they churned through the puddles. Airborne, the Lockheed banked, and flying low, skimmed the hangar roof in a parting salute to those who had helped and come to see us off.

As we flew west above the Michigan countryside, a panorama of green fields made an even deeper shade by the dark skies, it just did not seem possible we were going to fly around the world. Why, this was just like a regular flight to South Bend—except that our destination this evening was Oakland, California, 2100 miles from Willow Run and the starting point of Earhart's flight.

When Polhemus had first contacted Collins Radio there had been talk of using the facilities of their "radio shack" for communications with the States. However, shortly afterward we had been notified that this would not be permitted. But when Colonel Payne came aboard, he arranged not only for us to use Liberty Airways, the call sign for the Collins station, but also the Andrews Presidential station located outside Washington, D.C. Our call sign for this HF network was "Rapid Rocket," suggested by Polhemus and a pun indeed considering indicated airspeed was 135 mph.

Payne turned his transmit switch to the HF position. "Andrews. Andrews," he called. "This is Rapid Rocket. Do you read?"

There was no reply. He tried again. Still no answer.

Lee was sitting in the navigator's seat, frowning.

"Try tuning to 15 megacycles," Payne told him. "That's

the international time signal. The identification is WWV."

Lee switched frequencies and the steady ticking of the time signal was heard along with the Morse code identifiers for the letters WWV.

"Did you check the installation?" I asked Lee. "No loose wires or anything?"

"We followed the diagrams so closely, and yet. . . ."

"The power supply," I prompted.

"The converters are putting out what they should be."

"The switches?"

"Positioned correctly. Guess we'll stop at Collins Radio and see if they can find the trouble."

The HF was not working properly. More delay! Until it functioned, we could not continue.

Our groundspeed to South Bend was 121 mph. At that speed, the flight time to Oakland was 16 hours—not including fuel stops.

Over Lake Michigan the sun peeked through the overcast, momentarily sending shafts of light darting on the ripples below. West of Chicago our groundspeed rose to 123 mph, but ahead the horizon was dark, not a local thunderstorm we could circumnavigate, but a solid squall line. We landed at DuPage County Airport to wait out the storm. Payne called Collins Radio and they said someone would be waiting when we arrived.

At 3:05 the wheels touched the runway at Cedar Rapids. No sooner had the propellers stopped than Collins's chief trouble shooter, Ken Roland, climbed aboard. He and Lee rechecked the installation.

After talking with a reporter and then returning some telephone calls, I went back to the Lockheed. No one was there—even the 618-T3 was gone. I traced men and radio to the test shop where Lee and Payne were sitting dejectedly on a bench waiting for the results of the radio check. In a few minutes Mr. Roland said, "Nothing wrong with the set. Let's go back to the plane."

The wiring was rechecked. Finally the trouble was located—one missing wire! It was quickly installed.

After supper we flew the plane to test the radio. Lee let out the trailing antenna.

"Andrews. Andrews. This is Rapid Rocket. Do you read?" queried Payne from the cockpit.

No sooner had he stopped transmitting than I heard, "Rapid Rocket. Rapid Rocket. This is Andrews. We read you five by five."

Were we really talking to a station just outside Washington, D.C? It seemed incredible, accustomed as I was to line-of-sight transmissions on our VHF equipment.

From the navigator's station, Mr. Roland transmitted, "Liberty Airways. This is Rapid Rocket. Do you read?"

"Rapid Rocket. Liberty Airways reads you loud and clear."

The HF worked! The flight could continue!

After we landed, Lee called his wife. He had forgotten his passport, the elevator gust locks, and the box of spare landing gear fuses. Polhemus was to bring these items to Miami.

I sent a telegram to Thornton and Thornridge high schools—that money would pay for our hotel rooms tonight. By nine o'clock the additional messages had been acknowledged, more calls returned, and the Lockheed tucked under the wing of the Collins Corporation airplane in the company hangar.

At the hotel, rain blew against the windowpanes, lightning blazed, and thunder boomed. I jumped into a hot shower and gradually a soothing tiredness replaced the tenseness. The bed looked inviting, the pillow soft. Crawling in, I thought—"How are we going to arrive over Howland on time? Already another day has been lost. I must remember to ask Don to query Shell Oil Company about deferring payments until at least September." The bill for this stop had been $51.54.

At the same time that it had been costly, the stop at Cedar Rapids had been valuable to me in more ways than one. Not only was the HF now working properly so that we might continue our flight in the morning, but also I had been treated to a very informative conversation at dinner. Heinz Blankenhagen, in charge of radio operations at the Collins "radio shack," had explained the HF SSB (single sideband) system of communication. After listening to him I had a far better understanding and a real appreciation of the radio with which Collins had equipped us. The knowledge that Collins Corporation was largely responsible for the technological developments which now made the HF SSB radio the dominant mode of long-range communication further increased my respect for our patron.

Although at the time of Earhart's flight the theory of HF SSB communication was well understood, practical, technological, and economic difficulties hindered its application. How glad I was that this was 1967 instead of 1937, and that our plane, although a sistership of Earhart's, testified in its equipment to thirty years of progress.

At 7:15 the next morning we left Cedar Rapids. Soon shimmering fleecy clouds were below us and the sun was blazing behind. Lee tuned the Collins to the suggested primary frequency for contacting Andrews.

"Andrews. Andrews," Payne said. "This is Rapid Rocket. How do you read?"

"Loud and clear," crackled over the headset.

"Off Cedar Rapids at 1215 Zulu," continued Bill. "Estimating Oakland, California, June 9 at 0200 Zulu with a fuel stop at Ogden, Utah."

"Copied and will stand by," said Andrews.

Zulu, or Greenwich time, is used for flight logs to avoid the complications and confusion which would result from the use of various time zones. I decided to keep my watch on Eastern Daylight Saving time so that by adding four hours, I would always know what time it was on the Greenwich meridian. Local times could be found by adding or subtracting the correct number of hours. More probably, I would look at a clock after we landed.

After checking in with Liberty Airways, we opened the breakfast box Collins had provided. The rolls were soft, the milk cold, and the apples juicy. What great assistance these Collins people had provided—loaning us the transceiver, finding the reason the set hadn't worked, and providing our en route breakfast.

At 7:41 Andrews called again, "Rapid Rocket. Rapid Rocket. Radio check."

"Loud and clear," Payne replied. He grinned, crinkles forming around his clear blue eyes. "This HF stuff coupled with single sideband is amazing. Almost unbelievable how far these signals propagate."

After my talk with Heinz, how well I understood Payne's comment.

Payne took a small plastic container from a zippered pocket on the left shoulder of his flight suit, removed a pair of ear plugs, and inserted them. "Mine are medium sized," he said. "I brought a small set for you and medium ones for Lee and Polhemus.

My ears were still ringing from the flight yesterday and a dull heavy ache at the back of my head hadn't vanished with sleep. In fact, the noise level from the engines was almost a disconcerting factor. The ear plugs and headset made the noise bearable. Lee elected not to use the plugs because it was considerably quieter in the cabin, so Payne carefully screwed the cap on the container and put it back in the pocket, closing the zipper.

When I wanted to talk to Payne, I tapped his shoulder and we both leaned toward the center of the cockpit. I pulled the left earpiece of his headset away from his ear and shouted. That was conversation in the cockpit of our Lockheed 10!

Over Nebraska clouds began building, some becoming thunderstorms which we detoured. Groundspeed was a respectable 154 mph, the result of tailwinds more than of increased speed of the plane. Lee came forward and stood in the cockpit-door opening. "Think we should transfer fuel now?" he asked. "The mains are about half empty."

Payne nodded and Lee moved the selector switch to pump fuel from the forward fuselage tanks into the main wing tanks. Then he activated two of the electric fuel pumps on each side, the ones operating from the plane's electrical system and not on the auxiliary batteries. The pumps chattered softly.

"Keep an eye on the main-tank-fuel gauges," Lee said.

Slowly the needles crept around the dial as more gas was

pumped into the tanks than the engines were using. When the mains were nearly full, Lee stopped the pumps. Then he flew while I sat at the nav station and updated my personal log of the flight and the record sheets for the movie and still film.

The pass through the mountains directly east of Ogden was blocked by a storm so we flew north along the eastern side of the range to another pass. "There it is," Payne said, pointing to a gap in the mountains. "Let me know if you see a road and river on your side after we enter. Not much room to turn around if this isn't the right one."

After the Lockheed had entered the narrow gorge, I confirmed the river and road snaking along the bottom. Mountains on both sides and clouds covering the peaks crowded us until I wanted to fold the wingtips. Hoping the western end was not blocked, we followed curve after curve until finally a wide valley was ahead. Turning south toward Ogden, we informed Andrews that we would be off the air for an hour and would contact them when we were airborne again.

Fueling. Reporters. Telephone calls. Hot coffee and doughnuts. Then we departed for Oakland.

After landing at Ogden, I had put my ear plugs on top of the instrument panel. Now only one was there. Payne located the other one beneath my seat. Without these plugs I would have had a continuous headache, not to mention the effect of the noise on my eardrums. Payne was lucky to have that flight suit with the many pockets. Next time my plugs would be put away in his plastic container.

Purple twilight hovered as we caught sight of the green and white flashes of the rotating beacon at Oakland International. After landing, we taxied to the old airport from where Earhart had departed, stopping in front of the transient terminal. Payne put his ear plugs away and I dropped mine on top of his. After talking with newsmen, returning some phone calls, and contacting Don and Polhemus, I was ready for sleep—a day at least—but at the motel were more calls to be returned. The phone practically fell from my hand as the last one was completed. It had been a long day—almost fourteen hours of flying—but we were in Oakland.

EXCHANGING flight covers with Elmer H. Dimity, President of the Amelia Earhart Foundation, who had loaded Earhart's covers aboard in 1937.

June 9 began under an overcast sky with a damp chilly wind blowing off San Francisco Bay, but the warm reception we received from the people who had come to see us off more than compensated. Whenever I talked with one person, others crowded around, jotting notes or pushing still another microphone among those already in the inner circle. Several people had witnessed Earhart's take off. One was Elmer H. Dimity, president of the Amelia Earhart Foundation, who had put Earhart's flight covers aboard. He handed me a sample of her covers and I gave him one of ours.

Everyone, including Fred Goerner whose book in one sense had started all this, wanted to know my ideas about the fate of Amelia Earhart. I told them the flight was to commemorate the thirtieth anniversary of the earlier one, but if something did turn up. . . .

By ten o'clock the flight covers had not come back from being cancelled. We couldn't leave without them, so our flight plan departure time was extended to 10:30. When the boxes of covers arrived, Lee and I carried them to the wing lockers. Payne was already in the cockpit when I scrambled into the pilot's seat.

"Will you stand up in the hatch?" a newsman asked.

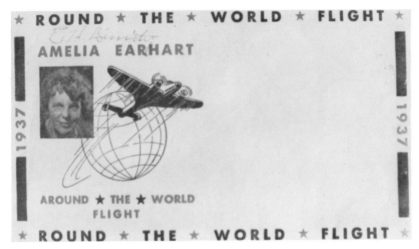

SAMPLE of the flight cover carried by Amelia Earhart. This cover was signed and given to me by Elmer Dimity.

This time waving was easier—I was really waving good-bye! Then I turned the tables on the news media people. "How about you people waving and smiling for a change?" They complied and the moment was recorded on slide and movie film.

"Ready now?" asked Payne.

ONE OF OUR flight covers from Lae, New Guinea, showing the special commemorative cancellation used there.

DEPARTING OAKLAND, June 9, 1967. On the Earhart Trail at last! (Courtesy Port of Oakland)

I sat down, being careful not to crush the white orchid Mr. Kilpatrick from the Oakland Port Authority had pinned on my jacket, and started the engines. Ground Control cleared us to the same runway Earhart had used and then requested that we delay take off until the cameras had been positioned alongside the runway. At 10:45 everything was ready. As this airplane's sistership had done thirty years ago, our Lockheed moved down the runway. The wheels lifted and we were on the Earhart Trail, a trail which led back thirty years, but also forward and around the world.

Halfway to Tucson raw gasoline fumes filled the plane. The fuel pumps were stopped and the visible seams on the tanks inspected. They were dry with no signs of the red dye used in 80-87 octane fuel. Were the lines leaking? Had a seam split underneath? Had the tanks shifted enough while we were flying through rough air yesterday to put a strain on a seam? Lee spotted a red stain trailing back from the filler cap on the right wing tank. Both main wing tank gauges indicated FULL.

"Guess I overfilled the tanks," Lee said. "Should have watched the process more closely."

We all agreed to watch the process more closely next time!

About midnight, after eleven hours total flying time and an intermediate fuel stop at Tucson, we landed at Greater Southwest Airport near Fort Worth. Originally, our flight plan had called for a fuel stop at Houston where Earhart had landed, but A & A's offer to donate gasoline and their facilities at Greater Southwest changed our minds.

The next day during our fuel stop at New Orleans, we experienced the first of many pleasant contacts with Pan American Airways personnel. PAA had agreed to assist with fuel and overnight accommodations and to provide box lunches and flight briefings when we landed where one of their facilities was located. In turn, we would be billed for these services.

At 8:30 we landed at Opa Locka Airport near Miami, and taxied to the A & A facility where we had been offered free use of fuel and facilities—our reason for not landing at Miami International where the PAA facility was and where Earhart had landed.

Don had flown down commercially with Polhemus and his wife Jan. They had more than a hundred pounds overweight luggage charge, but the vacuum pump had been forgotten. An oil leak had developed on the pump on the right engine and since Lee had a spare one he wanted to install it. Immediately he called Detroit and arranged for it to be flown down on the next freight flight with special handling.

After talking with the news-media people, I went to the motel where Don and Polhemus were waiting.

The first thing Polhemus asked was, "Do you have my shot record?"

"Here in my purse," I told him. "I picked up yours, Lee's, and mine at the hospital on Monday when I paid the bill."

"Well," Polhemus began, "when I arrived from London, they wouldn't let me in the country until I had another vaccination."

At least we would not have to worry about catching smallpox from him during the flight!

After dinner Don changed into work clothes and left for Miami International to track down the vacuum pump. Then he and Lee worked until 4:00 a.m. installing it. When Don returned to the motel room, he pointed to the two piles of items on the floor.

"What are those?" he asked.

"The items in the larger pile are for you to take back to Michigan. When I saw Polhemus had brought those two big chart cases, the elevator locks, that carton of miscellany, his suitcase and hanging bag, I thought about how overweight the plane would be and decided to send back absolutely everything I could do without."

The crew was now complete. I looked forward to the Caribbean!

SAN JUAN
CARACAS
TRINIDAD

★
  ★
★

THE NEXT MORNING A & A gave us enough fuel to bring our load to 450 gallons—250 in the wing tanks, 180 in the two forward fuselage tanks, and 20 in the rear fuselage tanks. Take-off weight was computed at 11,700 pounds, 1200 pounds over normal gross.

When the television interviews had been completed and Payne and Polhemus returned from filing our first international flight plan, good-byes were quickly said.

The air was humid and the temperature rising, factors which would make the Lockheed less efficient on take off. Although a slight wind favored another runway, the longest one was chosen. At 10:30 a.m. we started rolling and used more than half of the eight thousand feet before the plane rose sluggishly and inched upward, skimming the trees at the far end.

To the east lay the broad panorama of Miami and the Atlantic Ocean, dotted with splashes of sunlight between the storm clouds. Four minutes later we crossed the coastline, heading for Bimini Island. However, we were forced to change course because a storm blocked the direct route.

When we tried to call Miami Oceanic Control on their assigned frequency, no reply was received. Finally Payne called our time off and estimated time of penetrating the Air Defense Identification Zone to Andrews and they relayed the message. The HF reception was scratchy and "weak but readable."

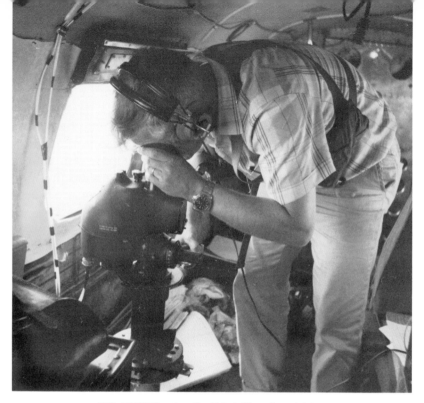

POLHEMUS using the B-3 drift meter which was gyrostabilized and superior to Noonan's.

Polhemus gave me a revised estimate for Yankee 1, a reporting point on our airway to San Juan. "It's eight minutes later than flight planned," he said. "All this off-course flying and dodging the rain have really reduced our groundspeed." Since we had flown beneath the clouds, Polhemus had been unable to use the sextant and had relied upon dead reckoning and the drift meter.

Signals were still weak when our change in ETA (estimated time of arrival) was radioed to Miami Oceanic via Andrews. Yet a half hour later we changed frequencies, and transmissions were loud and clear both ways with Andrews. How whimsically these waves seemed to propagate—voices sounded sometimes as though they were just outside the cockpit and other times as though on a distant planet.

Our first landfall was Andros Island, 35 miles wide. Long before it was due to creep over the horizon, I watched for it, feeling akin to the ancient mariner who had watched land rise from an endless blue ocean and grow larger until his ship lay safely in the harbor.

Polhemus came forward to join us in scanning the waters ahead. To stay underneath the rain clouds we sometimes flew as low as 300 feet above the water. Andros appeared, a faint elongated smudge, but as we flew closer, the shoreline and inlets became distinct. We "coasted on" (flew over the coast) twelve miles south of our intended landfall.

En route to Fowl Cay, the ocean, sky, and clouds provided an ever-changing seascape, complete with threat of storms. Ahead the horizon would be dark, but off one wingtip cumulous clouds puffed upward with sunlight between. Momentarily the plane would be in these clear areas, but when we flew under the fringes of storm clouds, the blues and greens of the waters became darker. Schools of fish swept silently beneath us, and ships trailed white wakes.

"I sure give Earhart a lot of credit for trying this in 1937," Polhemus said over the interphone.

I couldn't help thinking that although much had changed in thirty years, the water, weather, and islands here remained essentially the same.

Southeast of Long Island the rainstorms stopped and the sea and islands began to resemble the Caribbean travel posters. Polhemus shot the sun with the sextant and a few minutes later said we were 4 miles off Mayaguana Island. Visually, we proved this correct. It was voted to set the clock on the instrument panel to Zulu time, so Polhemus listened to WWV and called the correct time to us.

Near Caicos Island he tuned the radio compass, automatic direction finder, to San Juan's radio beacon some 340 miles away. The Morse code identifier came over the headphones and the needle steadied on zero, meaning San Juan was directly ahead. It was good to know the KR-80 ADF that King Radio had given us possessed this capability.

Occasionally, I sat on the rear edge of the fuselage tanks, fascinated by Polhemus's work with rows of figures, the sextant, a square plotter, and dividers. Now at 5500 feet, our groundspeed checked at 133 mph.

POLHEMUS transmits from nav station. Partially obscured by his hand is the Loran set. In the rear are the Collins "black boxes." Instruments on the panel are: airspeed, altimeter, remote indicating compass, omni head connected to VOR 1 in cockpit, ADF, and Collins tuning panel.

In my journal I wrote: "Everyone is tired except Polhemus. He works constantly, apparently enjoying it. He keeps our spirits up and we can almost forget how tired we are. He sings, He whistles. He points out interesting sights and gives a running commentary."

Polhemus asked if I wanted to use the drift meter. I nodded, so he turned the inverter on. Its high whine rang through the fuselage. Then he threw a switch on the navigator's panel which sent 110-volt AC to the B-3 gyro motor.

"Look through the eyepiece," Polhemus instructed. "Turn the adjusting knob until a white cap appears to move down and parallel to those red lines."

The whitecaps either did not stay in one place long enough or disappeared off the scope. By the time I had one lined up, another one was already moving down. Finally, they were moving parallel with the red lines.

"Now read the scale on the azimuth surrounding the meter," said Polhemus.

"Seven degrees right drift," I told him. So that was how a B-3 worked!

Now that we were over open sea, the storms and landfalls past, Lee slept, exhausted from staying up the previous two nights working on the Lockheed.

Polhemus radioed our ETA and twenty minutes before that time we started descending toward San Juan International, 1140 miles and eight and a half flying hours from Miami.

We taxied to the Pan American gate as directed by the tower and were met by PAA personnel who inquired what we would need in addition to accommodations which had been arranged. Lee and Polhemus stayed to fuel the plane and then taxi it to the overnight tie-down spot.

Payne and I took a taxi to the hotel. When I wanted to tip the bellhop in my room, my wallet was missing. Not even out of the States one day and I had lost my wallet!

"Look carefully through your purse," Payne said calmly. "Try to remember where you last saw it."

"Downstairs at the desk."

"I'll wait here while you retrace your steps," Payne said.

Dejectedly, I rode downstairs in the same elevator and followed the carpet to the desk. The hotel personnel had seen no wallet.

Credit cards gone. Flying licenses. Driver's license. Pictures. I felt very alone.

Back in my room the bellhop suggested, "Perhaps you should check all your luggage."

I unzipped my suitcase. No wallet. Then the small camera case. There was my wallet. While putting the Instamatic away downstairs, I must have absent-mindedly slipped the wallet inside too.

The alarm rang at five o'clock the next morning. I struggled out of bed, wanting to close my eyes and curl up again. But not today—today we were flying to Caracas and Paramaribo! By six o'clock we were at Pan American operations where Bob Tompkins took us for a weather briefing, assisted in filing our international flight plan, and ordered box lunches which would also serve as breakfast. General declarations for customs at Caracas were filled out in triplicate on PAA's official forms. Bob then drafted a cable to be sent as far as Dakar on the PAA circuit. Included were requests for hotel accommodations, food, fueling, and other miscellaneous services. On the PAA flight board we were listed as a SPECIAL departing at 8:00.

Bob drove us to the Lockheed. On the way Polhemus complained good naturedly, "I haven't had my morning coffee and there isn't any in the plane."

Already he had given up smoking his pipe because of the fuselage tanks. But coffee too—especially morning coffee?

"Why don't you just smile at one of those stewardesses in these jets and ask for a cup of coffee," I suggested.

Polhemus smiled wryly and shook his head.

Lee had checked the new vacuum pump and reported no oil leaking. Now he had the long hose from the fuselage tanks out the door and was draining some gasoline to check for water.

Two PAA mechanics walked over. "Are you Pellegreno on the Earhart flight? We saw the article in 'Sport Aviation.' "

I nodded.

"I'm Eddie Cruz and this is Eduardo Lugo Lugo. We're two thirds of the Experimental Aircraft Association in Puerto Rico. We're building a plane and majoring an engine like the one in your Miniplane. Maybe you can give us some tips on doing it."

I told them what had to be done on the engine and then showed them the interior of the Lockheed.

"So much equipment in such a little plane," Eduardo said. "Just like our jets."

"Not quite," I replied. "The Lockheed is a little slower."

After we had started the engines, there was a pounding on the fuselage door. Lee opened it. Bob Tompkins handed Polhemus a steaming coffeepot and a cup!

The flight to Caracas was 562 miles, mostly over open water. Since mountains rise to over 4000 feet on Puerto Rico, we circled off the northern coast to gain altitude before starting south. After leaving the island, we flew southwest until we reached 67 degrees west longitude and 17 degrees north latitude. To have turned south immediately would have put us inside the Atlantic Weapons Range Bravo, a restricted and potentially dangerous area. I doubt that Earhart had this type of problem! We were encountering but one of the many flight restrictions the government and military have imposed during the last thirty years.

A hazy atmosphere prevailed between the huge soft-edged cumulous clouds making visibility less than we would have liked at our cruising altitude of 6000 feet. We had found it advantageous to climb to at least 5000 feet because parasitic drag (antennas, round-head rivets, etc.) was less in the thinner air.

Generally, reception on the HF was loud and clear except for the several times transmission and reception had been blanked out. Personnel at Liberty Airways said the antenna had "loaded up" when this occurred and advised switching to a lower frequency and keying the microphone for several seconds which would clear the antenna so operation could be resumed on the primary frequency.

Polhemus used the sextant to run a sun line of position, the same technique with which we would attempt to locate Howland Island and the technique Noonan probably had been using.

The flight log columns filled with MPP's (most probable position) and ETA's for the assigned reporting points which were coordinates of longitude and latitude over water. We reported into the Curacao Flight Information Region (FIR) and Oceanic Control (CTA), talking directly and not relaying via Andrews.

Thirty-two miles from Maiquitia Airport located on the Venezuelan coast near Caracas which is inland behind the first mountain range, radar began vectoring us to final approach. A 20-knot wind was blowing directly down the runway and the Lockheed touched slower than usual, rolling quickly to a stop. After a flight of four hours and twenty minutes, we stepped from the plane to be welcomed by Gordon Jaquis from Champion, Francisco Corral from the J. Walter Thompson Agency which worked in connection with Champion, PAA personnel, newsmen, photographers, and Mrs. Rivas and her son Quito who were friends of Evelyn Kaiser. A two-day stay had been planned with a tour of the city, dinners, and visits to local flying clubs. Unfortunately, the time element dictated a two-hour stop, sufficient only for fueling and food. Gasoline was delivered in liters, so Polhemus and Lee used conversion tables to figure an equivalent amount in U.S. gallons.

The reporters knew a little English and I knew a little Spanish, but eventually one of the photographers acted as an interpreter. Then in the terminal restaurant Mrs. Rivas treated us to cold lemonades which eased the parched feeling in my throat, the result of being in the hot wind and sun for more than an hour. The wind also prompted my decision to forget about my hairdo and just be the "tousle-haired blond" the newspapers called me.

With some regret, we said good-bye to our Venezuelan friends—and I do call them friends, because there is something about air travel and travelers that cements friendships almost instantaneously. But, Paramaribo was 882 miles away and tropical storms, prevalent and occurring quite regularly in this region and season during the afternoons, were forecast. Our plan was to attempt the inland route across Venezuela, staying north over the water until the mountain ranges were lower.

For seventeen minutes we climbed slowly and steadily to 5000 feet. On our right steep mountains stood erect—one peak towering into the clouds at over 9000 feet—even as they stubbed the toes of their dark green feet in the sea.

An hour and a half later, we turned inland, crossing the 2000-foot mountains easily. I hoped the inland route would be clear because now between us and the relative safety of the sea lay mountains gradually rising to more than 8000 feet.

Polhemus circled the small village of El Pilar on his chart. A short while later a thunderstorm swirled in moving almost as fast as the Lockheed, so we flew parallel to and south of the coastal ranges hoping for a break in the solid rain ahead. Below, the land looked much the same—small winding rivers, a few meandering roads, and no distinct landmarks on the rolling hills. Without the sextant, useless now because of clouds above, we relied mainly on pilotage, comparing the charts with the terrain.

Eighty miles from where we had started inland, we began our devious route to the ocean to escape the storm. Tentatively, we entered the mountains, watching the clouds above and the rapidly rising land below. Mountains surrounded us. When a ridge appeared ahead, we climbed slightly, hoping the clouds would not close the gap before we got there. When a valley angled in the general direction of our flight path, we followed it. Reminders of the pass east of Ogden! There were absolutely no airports in this area and to the south lay miles of vast emptiness. The higher the mountains rose, the more we climbed to follow their sloping valleys. Flying through a particularly narrow one, Polhemus commented, "The jaguars are looking down on us!" Soon we were looking for the "wild animals"and imitating Polhemus's pronunciation—an exaggerated JAG-U-ARS!

Finally, the Lockheed topped the last ridge. Beyond was a wide marshy plain and in the distance the Gulf of Paria. We followed a river toward it and then flew along the Peninsula de Paria, that long arm of Venezuela which extends toward Trinidad.

Polhemus replotted our course to Paramaribo, but when we "coasted off" (left the coast of) the eastern edge of Trinidad, he said, "Our groundspeed has fallen to 113. We've picked up a terrific headwind."

Puzzled, he rechecked his calculations, but arrived at the same low number. Dusk came and then darkness. Polhemus wanted to shoot a three-star fix to confirm our position, so I handed him the Air Almanac and the Sight Reduction Tables. He transferred figures from these to a star-sighting sheet, using a time several minutes hence when he would be shooting the stars. During daylight hours the sextant required no current because the bubble was visible in the chamber, but at night a bubble light was needed. Polhemus pushed the sextant into the mount, flipped the inverter switch, and then looked into the eyepiece.

"Now what's wrong with the bubble light," he grumbled. "Let's try the cable from the other sextant." He crawled forward on the fuselage tanks, opened the other box, and whipped out the cable. After he had attached it, the bubble light still didn't work. The time for the "shot" approached.

"Give me a flashlight," he said, as he began unscrewing the cap which covered the sextant light. Suddenly, the cap fell. Polhemus muttered as he looked for it on the floor. I grabbed another flashlight, found the cap, and handed it to him.

"Where's my small screwdriver? I need it to get the little bulb out." He found it at the bottom of his briefcase. Seconds later the tiny bulb was on the floor.

"Darn," muttered Polhemus. "I've already missed my sighting time. We may be in trouble if those headwinds we picked up over Trinidad continue."

I picked up the bulb and it was replaced in the sextant. Then Polhemus inserted the extra sextant in the mount. The bubble light worked perfectly.

Polhemus preplanned another star shot. Then he twirled the pre-set knobs on the sextant to line up the coordinates for the first star and looked into the eyepiece. "We must be under an overcast," he said. A look out the window confirmed this. He continued, "Now you can imagine the difficulty Noonan would have had with a hand-held bubble octant in perhaps turbulent air. Maybe those two could rely on nothing but dead reckoning over the Pacific where an overcast would have been especially serious. And what if we had left one sextant in the wing locker and carried the inoperative one inside?"

"It could be bad," I agreed.

Polhemus calculated the remainder of the flight using the last known groundspeed. "I think we'll have to return to Trinidad," he said. "Our ETA at Paramaribo is in four hours, the same time our fuel will be exhausted. Too risky to continue."

"Whatever you say, Navigator," I told him although disappointed over the further delay.

"Turn to 320 degrees," said Polhemus. The Electra, engines droning, raised its right wing and turned obediently in response to control pressures.

With an amended flight plan calling for a landing on Trinidad, we "homed" on the radio beacon at Piarco International Airport over which we had flown earlier, heading in the opposite direction.

After the wheels touched the runway gently, the tower directed us to park by the terminal. Moments later the Shell gasoline truck arrived. To add to our problems, the man said fuel was delivered in Imperial gallons. We postponed fueling until morning as we had not decided whether to stop at Paramaribo or fly straight through to Belem.

The Shell man checked inside the terminal for PAA personnel. None was there; however, no alert cable had been sent. As we wasted the next two hours, we appreciated all the more what PAA had done for us at other stops. Without the help of the Shell man as we proceeded slowly through British formalities at night at a non-scheduled stop, we might never have left Trinidad!

Payne had been searching through his luggage. "I can't find my passport," he told me. "I thought I put it in the pocket of my flight suit."

"Now, when was the last time you remember seeing it?" I asked, reversing the roles we had played in San Juan. "Let's look through everything carefully."

We checked the bottom of his hanging suit bag and his small travel case. No passport. Without it we would be delayed here until another could be obtained.

"Look through all the pockets in your suit," I suggested.

Payne pulled his passport from an inside pocket of the jacket.

"Must have put it there when we went out for dinner last night and forgot to transfer it to my flight suit."

"That was a close one," I agreed.

"Why don't you look after my passport for a while?" Payne said and tucked it in my purse. My extremely efficient and capable copilot was asking me to look after his passport!

The first stop inside the terminal was Health, or "Sanidad," as was posted above the desk. Here we convinced the man our plane had been fumigated en route. This turned out to be the only item on the checklist which did not require time or money. He then looked sleepily at our shot records, going over each one an interminable length of time. I'm not sure how much he saw as his eyes appeared bloodshot and not from lack of sleep!

When he finally returned our records, we followed the Shell man to customs. The man there would not accept the general declarations made out for Paramaribo and handed me an entirely new set which I filled out quickly. He investigated our suitcases, map cases, and hanging bags.

At Immigration, I knocked on the closed door. Nothing happened. I banged louder. A few minutes later the door opened. Behind the man I could see a card game in progress. Smoke filled the room and bottles were on the table, but when I thought what these men were probably paid in return for the long hours, I didn't blame them a bit.

He looked at our passports, and looked again. The odor of rum was noticeable. Finally, he stamped our papers and we left the terminal for the motel accommodations the Shell man had arranged.

At the motel I looked at the Trinidad gray sheets, hoped the bugs would stay in their places on the floor and ceiling, and curled up inside my bathrobe which was clean.

BELEM
NATAL
DAKAR

THE NEXT MORNING WE ARRIVED at the airport with the knowledge that the men from customs, health, and immigration were "building churches" and a contribution would speed processes. Sure enough, in the health officer's shirt pocket was a small envelope.

"I hear you're building a church," Payne said politely and smiled.

"Yes," the man replied. "I need money. Building costs a lot."

Payne gave him two dollars, discreetly folded. The man thanked him and with much obviousness opened the envelope and tucked the money beside a single bill probably put there for bait and authenticity. At Immigration another church was being built, so I contributed. No doubt this money went for "liquid churches" but it was worth the time saved, as our forms were initialed and stamped immediately with no fuss. Someday it would be interesting to ask one of these men to take us on a tour of the island. Certainly there should be some very beautiful buildings.

A $9 landing fee which was based on gross weight was paid at the airport manager's office. The "official" parts of leaving taken care of, it was time to turn to more practical things such as weather, food, and fuel. On the previous evening's weather chart appeared the wall of wind that had forced our return to Trinidad. Wind arrows at 7000 feet and up had four barbs, one for each ten knots of wind!

The forecast for today, June 13, looked better, but thunderstorm activity was predicted along the Brazilian coast.

Polhemus warned that if our sextant could not be fixed, we might have to wait at Natal until another could be shipped from Kollsman. This delay would cost our objective—Howland Island thirty years later!

Parked next to the Lockheed was a four-engine military plane. Reasoning that a plane of this size had a navigator, I explained our flight, and asked advice on the sextant. The navigator accompanied me to the Lockheed where I opened the case containing the troublesome instrument.

"We use the same kind," the navigator said. "Let me take it to our plane and check it."

I watched him disappear inside the cavernous hulk of the military plane. Finally, he returned.

"You'll find your sextant in perfect working order," he said and winked. "We have a daylight flight back to base today and ours can be repaired before we fly at night."

When Polhemus returned from filing the flight plan, I told him we now had two working sextants. He was as amazed as I at the transaction. Somehow things have a way of working out even if some solutions are not exactly conventional and occur completely by chance!

The Lockheed, loaded one ton over normal, skimmed trees at the far end of the runway and continued low over the hills, climbing slowly to 500 feet before turning on course to Belem, 11 flying hours and 1264 miles away.

Occasionally, we flew over the shoreline of South America, but mostly we flew over the ocean, the land hidden by dense tropical storms. One detour around a large cell took us twenty miles seaward. Less than 200 miles from Belem, a towering storm rose ahead of us. Then, almost miraculously, a "saddle back" appeared and we climbed rapidly, topping the swirling clouds in that low spot. In the fading daylight I took pictures of the Amazon River, that huge waterway which drains most of the upper part of South America and was so well remembered from grade school geography books.

My crew had informed me that a dousing was due when I

crossed the equator for the first time, but fortunately they were busy and forgot. Earhart had also missed her initiation. She wrote, "But at the time the Electra's shadow passed over the mythical line we were both so occupied he (Noonan) quite forgot to duck me with the thermos bottle of cold water which he later confessed had been provided for the occasion." ("Last Flight")

René Watrin, PAA Station Manager at Belem, and Fernando Lisboa, the senior maintenance supervisor who had just received his license to work on DC-8's, met us. Getting off the plane, I carried the black camera case, the 16mm camera, the folder with the plane's papers, and my purse.

"May I please carry your suitcase," Fernando asked. "It is much too heavy for a little lady like you to carry."

"Suitcase. I don't have a suitcase." I told him politely. "But thank you anyway."

"No. I insist. That bag is too heavy for you." He pointed to my "suitcase."

"That's my purse. No need for you to carry that," I told him, laughing.

"But I want to. And that camera is too heavy also." Fernando relieved me of both items.

Newsmen were waiting and although it was dark, they took pictures. René led us inside the terminal for Health, Immigration, and Customs. Asked for proof of one million dollars public liability insurance, I explained that although our policy covered this amount, I did not have it with me. René vouched for us and our papers were stamped. Then he drove us to the hotel where he had made reservations. My crew and I rode up twelve floors in the unstable elevator. How much safer we were in a thirty-year-old airplane!

Before the bellhop and his female counterpart left my room the girl asked, "Agua sin or con gais?"

"What?" I was puzzled. "Agua" meant water. "Sin" meant without. "Con" meant with. But "gais"? Was it Portuguese for ice?

"Nada. Nada. Gracias." I told her.

When Payne emerged from his room ready for dinner, I asked him.

"Carbonated or non-carbonated," he informed me. "All drinking water is bottled. It is a mineral type and the gas, or "gais," makes it more palatable.

Lee had decided to sleep, so Payne, Polhemus, and I walked several blocks to the International Cafe. As unfair as it may seem, if a person speaks Portuguese, he can understand Spanish easily, whereas the reverse is not true. The menu was in Portuguese and the only word we understood was "omelette." There were three kinds. We ordered one of each by pointing to the items wanted when the waiter came. This way we could at least learn three words of Portuguese. When the food finally arrived, we were so hungry we divided up the omelettes, and promptly forgot to ask the waiter which was which. Could he have understood our question? He spoke only Portuguese. Shrimp! Cheese! Fish! We had our three omelettes, but our vocabulary for restaurants was still "omelette."

The next morning I was completely amazed—the cost of the four single rooms totaled $5.81 U.S.

Fernando was waiting in the PAA office and immediately took charge of my purse and camera. At the airport post office, he told me the correct stamp was not available for the flight covers, but a combination of two stamps would make the proper postage. I bought 1800 stamps, the entire stock, and enough for 900 of the 2000 covers which would be cancelled at Natal.

Box lunches included oranges, sandwiches, and four bottles of mineral water, one "sin gais" for Lee. "Gelo" would keep the water cold. I was glad the oranges were included, for at the airport restaurant they had served some of the freshest and most delicious orange juice I had ever tasted. One delight of the flight was having this kind of experience so far from home.

Fernando parted with my purse and camera reluctantly and as the plane thundered past him on take off, we dipped a wing in response to his wave.

At cruising altitude I asked Lee and Payne to fly, since I knew the task of stamping the envelopes awaited me. A captain, I believed, should not demand that her crew do what she

EN ROUTE from Belem to Natal: the tedious task of stamping the Brazilian flight covers.

would not. I sat in Lee's seat, separated the stamps, and then began the tedious task of affixing them. They were printed on thicker paper than that used in the United States and the glue was less than adequate. The sponge either dampened them too much or not enough and time was wasted. Therefore, to have just the right amount of moisture, I licked each stamp, keeping a cup of water nearby to rinse my mouth periodically. Brazilian glue was not mint flavored!

After yesterday, it was hard to believe so few clouds could exist—only scattered cumulus here and there and occasionally a high cirrus layer.

In the jungle east of Belem an occasional clearing appeared, a few dwellings with a dirt road winding past. Parts of the Brazilian interior are uncharted—some of this area as near as 50 miles to the coast. Notations on our charts read "level area data incomplete." Further inland were notices: "relief data incomplete."

Airports are hundreds of miles apart and the prospects of reaching one if trouble is encountered are slim indeed. The idea of landing in the jungle is downright terrifying! I would prefer ditching at sea where a chance of being seen by rescue parties exists!

Past San Luis, the sand stretched along the coast and inland—small dunes with ponds of still water between. Such interesting country and I was licking stamps! Polhemus, however, kept me informed about the terrain and our position. It must be somewhat frustrating for a navigator to sit anywhere but in the cockpit from where he can capture a broad view.

Passing Forteleza, where Earhart had landed, he pointed out the two airports. How strange that in a country so devoid of airports two hard-surfaced ones should be so close to a single city when one could have been placed to greater advantage near another city. Politics?

Most of the seven hours and twenty-five minutes to Natal I licked stamps. Lee came to my assistance near the end of the 1800 stamps. At six o'clock we landed at Natal, but before we had taxied to the Varig Airlines hangar it was dark. PAA had no office here but had arranged for Varig personnel to take care of us. But, again, a language problem. When we were leaving the plane, a young man arrived and said, "I'm Everaldo Porciuncula representing UPI."

"Everaldo, for heaven's sake, don't leave us. We can't speak Portuguese."

"Don't worry. I'll see that you have no problems. In fact, I'll accompany you to dinner."

After interpreting for the other newsmen, he left, promising to pick us up at the hotel at nine.

At the hotel I talked with still another newsman, then hurried to my room, and quickly took a cold shower, reminding myself how delightfully refreshing cold water could be.

Then I looked for my slip in the suitcase. It wasn't there and neither were my hose or white heels. In striving to save that extra pound for fuel, I had sent them home with Don from Miami. It was through mere forgetfulness I still had the dress.

In the rush of leaving, I had simply forgotten to give it to him.

Now the dress mocked me. Just how was I to dine at the choice restaurant in Natal wearing tennis shoes. Fortunately, I hadn't sent my white beads back. At least they helped create the illusion of being "dressed for dinner."

Everaldo drove us to the new hotel on the beach which was completely filled with representatives from other countries who had come to observe Brazil's first, in Everaldo's words, "rocket shoot" which would occur early the next morning.

For a change dinner was leisurely. Everaldo was extremely conversant and knowledgeable about Brazilian politics, the "rocket shoot," and his job as a reporter.

When we returned to the hotel at midnight, a note from a correspondent was waiting. I answered his questions first and then wrote my daily letter to Don.

Early the next morning horns blew, brakes screeched, vendors shouted, dogs barked, and newsboys hawked. Opening the shutters, I looked down over the red tiles of the sloping veranda roof to the intersection below where oblique rays of the morning sun made long slender shadows. Rush hour, Natal style. Sleep was now out of the question.

In a sunny second-floor room I devoured raised rolls with strawberry jam and butter, and coffee. Then I returned to my room and updated my flight journal.

I told my crew about breakfast procedures. Lee said he was going to work on the Lockheed all day. Payne and Polhemus were going to flight plan the Atlantic leg. No one was interested in helping with the flight covers and I hoped Everaldo would keep his promise of assistance.

Promptly at nine o'clock he pulled up to the hotel. "I was awake most of the night waiting for the 'rocket shoot' but they didn't fire it. Maybe tomorrow morning."

He was tired but still willing to help purchase stamps and stick them on the envelopes. The boxes of covers were in the plane so he drove me to the airport, nearly a half hour away, and helped carry them to the car.

At the Natal post office he talked to the woman selling stamps. She was reluctant to sell us the number required.

Finally, Everaldo persuaded her, but it was a lengthy process. The sheets came out one, sometimes two, at a time and were laid on the counter. The correct stamp was available here— seven cruzeiros for each envelope. When that supply was exhausted, we bought stamps valued at one, two, and three cruzeiros which we planned to combine. Everaldo figured the amount owed in U.S. dollars and I endorsed a traveler's check.

"Ask her about cancellation," I prompted him.

A few moments later he said, "She says none until this afternoon."

"We're leaving this afternoon," I objected.

Just then a voice behind us said, "I'm the postmaster here. Perhaps I can help."

Everaldo explained. The postmaster smiled. "Yes. I have a letter about these envelopes. Wait. I'll get the copy of the cable sent back."

He showed us the two messages and then said, "Don't worry about the cancellation. I have two men coming at 2:30 for your envelopes."

I left the envelopes already stamped at the post office and took the others to Everaldo's office where his brother Eraldo helped us for the next two hours. However, when we had finished, 300 stamps were left over. I had purchased the exact number needed. Where were the missing envelopes? They must still be in the Lockheed—the box Lee had been doing.

It was half-past twelve. Everaldo had some copy to write, so he called a cab and was soon putting the boxes of stamped envelopes on the back seat and giving the driver directions. Everaldo then promised to pick me up again at the hotel at two.

The old taxi, somehow running on at least half of its six cylinders, could have fallen apart any moment. It wheezed! It coughed! It shook! Somehow it maintained 25 mph through the winding streets of Natal, past the houses with their tile roofs. The road to the airport was two-lane concrete, but outside the city the surroundings were desolate. Halfway to the airport the engine quit. The driver looked back and shrugged. More time to be wasted! He opened the hood and tinkered with that amazing engine which must now be cajoled into running again. The sun glared on the road and heat surged through the open windows. Two cars passed going toward town. Fortunately, another taxi came en route to the airport, so the fare was split, and the boxes transferred. This driver waited until I had retrieved the missing envelopes from the plane and then drove me to the hotel.

The day was warm and humid. I took a shower, this time really relishing the cold water, and then packed my suitcase. There were advantages to traveling light—not much time was wasted packing and unpacking.

Everaldo arrived. We took the stamped envelopes to the post office and then put stamps on the remaining ones. The two men began cancellation—by hand—once on the stamp, another time on the envelope. This would take hours!

Everaldo drove me to a bank where a traveler's check was changed into cruzeiros to buy food for the Atlantic flight, and then dropped me at the hotel. My crew were checking out and had bought extra bottled water since no PAA water was available. The driver from Varig Airlines, who had brought Lee and the two Bills from the airport and would take them back, took me to the post office. Cancellation was progressing— the pile of finished envelopes was larger!

Everaldo had picked up his friend John who spoke no English but would accompany me to the market. At an open-air stall I picked out two bunches of bananas and some oranges. John chose the correct amount of money from my hand. I ate two bananas; that was lunch! In a small shop some rolls and mild cheese were wrapped in brown paper and tied with string. John was an extremely good sport about the entire venture although at his six-foot-three height, he didn't look exactly domestic carrying the bundles.

When we returned to the post office, the envelopes were finished. A beaming postmaster said, ''There, you see it is done in time.''

Barely in time as departure was scheduled for six o'clock and it was now after five. At the airport Lee loaded the flight covers and I stowed the food. Payne had filed the flight plan and was impatiently waiting for the clearance. We wanted to leave while some daylight remained, an advantage during the heaviest take off so far. The four wing tanks held 250 gallons, the two forward fuselage tanks 180 gallons, and the rear fuselage tanks held 350 of the 450 possible for a total of 780 gallons. This amount would give us a fuel endurance of 19.5 hours. Overgross weight was estimated at 13,300 pounds, 400 below our maximum allowable. Fuel accounted for 4680 pounds of this. I hoped the runway was long enough!

In an overweight configuration weight and balance are critical. With the rear fuselage tanks so full, the center of gravity was to the extreme rear of the limits.

The sun set. Still no clearance!

Earhart had taken off from Natal on a secondary grass runway because of a "perverse wind" blowing across the paved one. After receiving a weather briefing from the French who had two ships stationed in the South Atlantic, she and Noonan had walked the length of the sod with flashlights to "establish something in the way of guiding landmarks, however shadowy," before taking off at 3:15 a.m. ("Last Flight")

At 6:45 our clearance arrived. Five minutes later Lee was crouched behind the cockpit, his hand on the dump valve. The runway looked ridiculously short, for until the midway point it sloped upward and the remainder lay out of sight. Shuddering, I remembered the long take-off rolls at Miami and Trinidad. Now the plane was even heavier!

Though the engines were churning when the brakes were released, there was a pause before the plane started rolling. As slowly as a truck climbs a mountain in low gear, the Lockheed moved down the runway. I could have run faster!

The airspeed needle swung between 30 and 40. The tail remained firmly on the runway. There was absolutely no response from the elevators when the yoke was pushed forward. Then I saw the runway lights at the other end! The airspeed needle flicked to 50 and the tail rose slowly. Airspeed 60! The engines sent their steady thunder into the cockpit. 70! The green lights were coming closer and the plane showed no sign of wanting to fly. Then at 90 the plane staggered upward, propellers clawing at the unrelenting darkness. We climbed straight out until 200 feet separated us from the ground and then, banking gently, circled the airport to the right and flew north over Natal to the radio beacon, complying with the first part of the departure instructions. There we turned to 080 degrees and held that heading for two minutes before turning right to 118 degrees and flying for two minutes. Then—on course for Africa—55 degrees. Ahead was the Atlantic Ocean, 1875 miles of water, the ocean Columbus had crossed in ninety-two days and a space capsule in less than an hour. Our flight time was estimated at 15 hours and 10 minutes.

We were relieved when 1000 feet had been gained, but even then if an engine failed, the Lockheed might be almost in the ocean before we had dumped enough fuel to lighten the plane sufficiently.

In the confusion of leaving Ann Arbor, Polhemus had forgotten a chart which showed the proper projection of the Atlantic leg. Consequently, he had resorted to using a Pacific chart which covered the same latitude, and had simply renumbered the lines of longitude. Mapwise, the flight over the Atlantic began in the Solomon Islands!

For the first hour we cruised at 1000 feet using 30 inches of manifold pressure and indicating 112 mph. Even with full nose-down trim, forward pressure had to be held on the yoke because of the fuel in the rear fuselage tanks. Lee slept on the forward fuselage tanks, his torso on one side of the eleven-inch aisle and his knees on the other. If he, or anyone, sat in the rear seat during the first few hours, the airspeed dropped 10 miles per hour, that station being so far behind the center of gravity.

The weather forecast indicated thunderstorms in the vicinity of 5 degrees north latitude, a band of them lying along the intertropical front where towering cumulus breed in the moist unstable air.

Below us cloud banks stretched like rows of billowing sails, and between them the moon sent spangles dancing on the dark ocean. I liked this overwater flying, perhaps because it was only four of us and one old Lockheed against the ocean.

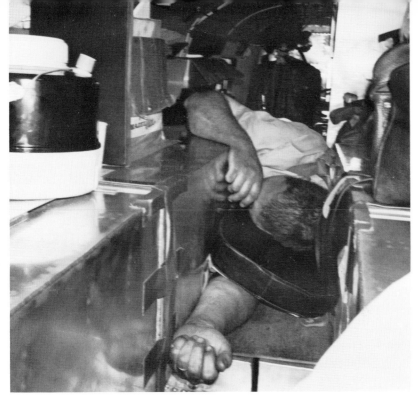

LEE SLEPT on forward fuselage tanks after overgross take off, but during second four hours he slept on the rear fuselage tanks where his torso didn't sag in the middle!

Position reports and radio chatter helped me stay awake. The following are some excerpts from my log.

0015 Zulu Received weather report from Liberty Airways for the rest of our flight tonight.

0030 Dakar forecast for our ETA is CAVU (ceiling and visibility unlimited).

0120 Ship passed to our right, heading west—its green nav light periodically disappearing as we fly over hazy clouds. Our altitude now 3000 feet.

0130 Clear now. Moon on wings and water.

0135 Polhemus shooting fix, the second one.

0145 Scattered cumulus. We fly through the tops and are bounced slightly from the rising currents. Bananas taste good.

0220   Fuel check. Estimating 47 gph (gallons per hour) so far, including climb. Thirteen hours and fifteen minutes remain. Running now at 250 bhp (brake horsepower).

0225   Polhemus just radioed our position via HF to Recife Oceanic Control.

0230   Moon disappearing behind clouds. Another banana.

0235   Overcast. Climbing for 5000 feet, but instead level off at 4000 which puts us above clouds.

0256   Another boat ahead. Darker now with moon gone.

Lightning flashed ahead, outlining the storms. My shoulder ached from holding in the right aileron continually, and it became increasingly difficult to remain alert. With no autopilot, this flight would have been impossible alone. Payne and I spelled each other, but even when not flying we had responsibilities—constant checking of fuel transfer, log entries, food, radio. Four hours after take off Lee moved to the rear fuselage tanks to sleep, since gas was pumped from them first.

Finally, I asked Payne to fly so I could take a short nap. My eyes just would not stay open. Still wearing the headphones, I put my pillow against the corner of the cockpit and settled against it. When we hit the storms I would wake up. Payne had started counting the turns of the crank which transferred oil from the nose tank into the right engine sump: 34, . . . 35, . . . 36, . . . 37, . . . 38. . . . The engines drummed their tireless rhythm.

Two hours later I awoke! Blue iridescent arcs of St. Elmo's fire outlined the tips of the propellers where they sliced through the charged atmosphere. Light rain spattered against the windows. Where were the storms?

"I slowed the plane to 115 because of the updrafts and downdrafts in the thunderstorms," Payne informed me. "Heavy rain too, but the plane didn't leak a drop!"

"I felt nothing! If you want to sleep, I'll fly," I told him.

Since the storms, Polhemus had been navigating by dead

reckoning because an overcast made star sights impossible; with a continent for a landfall we just continued flying toward Dakar, located on a peninsula jutting twenty miles into the Atlantic.

The hours passed as we flew through time and space, almost as if we were not a part of the earth, but alone. Only radio checks from Andrews and Liberty Airways broke the spell.

Polhemus slept. There were no landmarks on our route across the Atlantic, no island with a distinct shape, no atolls. The closest land was ocean bottom more than 2 miles below our wings.

The eastern sky lightened imperceptibly, or perhaps it was just an uncanny awareness that dawn was approaching. The rain stopped, the sky turned faint pink, and the red sphere which was the sun crested the horizon, leading forth daylight and gradually poking through the thin flat clouds lying close to the water to send dazzling rays into the cockpit.

Finally the clouds parted enough to allow a sextant shot. According to that, we were fifty miles right of course. Then the overcast returned, but the weather looked clear ahead and somewhere out there was the coast of Africa.

Less than an hour later we penetrated a storm. Rain cascaded down the windshield, encasing the plane in solid grayness and the controls jerked, the rate of climb zooming upward 2000 feet per minute. I eased back on the power, slowed the plane to 115. Then, as suddenly as the plane had been tossed upward, it plunged downward through the squally clouds.

"This is like the storms we flew through while you slept," Payne said.

The yoke and rudder pedals shuddered as the air currents played with the control surfaces. Then we were through the storm, the half-hour battle over.

Polhemus was able to take another shot and said we were off course to the east. A half hour later he took another sighting. Ninety miles east of course and 210 miles from Dakar was his estimate. That was almost directly south. A strong wind shift must have occurred, for our heading was 002 degrees, almost directly north. Headings throughout the night had ranged from 044 to 060 degrees, but if my navigator said, "Fly almost north," I would!

"J. P. McCarthy on the line," Polhemus called on the interphone. Before the flight I had been a guest on his radio show in Detroit. He had kept his listeners informed about our progress and now talked on a phone patch through Liberty Airways.

Whenever I spoke on the HF, I said words twice.

"Where are you, Annie?" asked J.P.

"Nearing Africa, Nearing Africa."

"How do you feel?"

"Very tired. Very tired."

"Tired, huh."

"Flew all night. Flew all night. Bad storms. Bad storms."

"You flew all night after being up all day yesterday?"

"Yes. Yes. Say hello to everyone. Say hello to everyone."

"Will do," said J.P. " 'Bye now. Good luck."

J. P.'s voice had come through loud and clear. A few minutes later I talked with Don, but the reception was faint and he barely understood my transmissions. Though tremendous advances have been made in radio communications since 1937, man still has not been able to control the atmosphere through which the waves must pass.

Our radio compass (ADF) needle was pointing to the Dakar beacon, confirming the off-course position estimate that the city was almost directly north. I could not help but think of Earhart going against her navigator's judgment and landing 125 miles north of Dakar at St. Louis.

My first glimpse of Africa, brown with patches of green, was through scattered clouds. The sun was bright overhead and the rains were behind us. As we descended from 7000 feet, warmth crept into the plane and soon we switched to the tower frequency.

"Trailing antenna in?" I asked Polhemus.

The long concrete runway was ahead and the wheels touched. At the terminal we shut the engines. Unbelievable silence! Four cold weary people climbed out after a 14 hour-and-10 minute flight.

DAKAR

AFRICA! DAKAR! Sunshine! A warm breeze!

Dressed impeccably in a light blue suit, Angelo Mezzadri, Airport Manager for PAA, greeted us as we alighted. "I've been expecting you. So have the newsmen who have gone to lunch."

He told us no cable had been received from AOPA regarding our alternate route across Africa, but one confirming the amount of insurance and the policy number had arrived.

Suddenly Lee stooped and looked underneath the fuselage. "We've lost the trailing antenna. Must have snagged it landing."

"My fault," said Polhemus. "I should have checked it. I remember Ann asking me to reel it in."

"No," I added, "the fault is mine. I should have confirmed that the wire had been rolled in."

The antenna footage meter indicated that 250 feet were still trailing. Mr. Mezzadri asked some PAA employees to search the area near the approach end of the runway.

Just then the newsmen returned from lunch and talked rapidly in French with Angelo. "They want to know if you will 'arrive again' since they waited so long before eating."

Remembering how helpful newsmen had been throughout the flight, I said, "Sure."

Lee removed the chocks. I started the engines and Payne explained our strange request to the ground controller who gave permission to taxi to the far edge of the ramp and "arrive

DAKAR: Angelo Mezzadri (right), PAA airport manager, confers with newsmen shortly after our arrival.

again" at the spot where we were now parked.

A few minutes later we were smiling and shaking hands with Mr. Mezzadri while our conversation which had been going on before the second "arrival" continued. Although several reporters spoke a little English, Angelo interpreted for them in addition to the ones who spoke no English.

One reporter came forward and looked at me for several seconds, holding up a piece of paper. "Are you Ann Pel-le-gre-no?" He pronounced the name carefully.

"Yes. You seem puzzled about something."

"I didn't think you would look like you do."

"Oh."

"The cable says you are a retired school teacher. I thought you would have gray hair."

"I did teach school, but last year decided to enter aviation full time."

The PAA truck returned. No antenna wire had been found. Fortunately, Don had coiled the wire from the hand-operated antenna reel which had been purchased before the electric one and insisted it be put in the box of spare parts. Without a trailing antenna the Collins HF and the Loran would not have worked properly.

Lee found the extra wire. "I'll put this on after lunch. But what will we use for a drag cone?"

"I ordered an extra one," Polhemus said. "The company was to ship it here. I'll check the freight office after lunch."

Customs took only a few minutes. Passports and shot records were in order and we were allowed into Senegal with little fuss. As we were going through the gates, a man said, "I'm the press attaché from the Russian embassy in Dakar."

"Karashaw, Gespadin," I greeted him in Russian. This however, was followed quickly by my saying that was the only phrase I knew in his language.

"What is the purpose of your flight?" he asked.

I told him about Amelia Earhart.

"Why not come to Moscow?"

"It's not on her route. Earhart wanted to fly as close to the equator as possible."

"Would you give me a statement for the newspaper I write in Russia?"

What did I want to say? I thought a moment and then told him, "You might say that it would be wonderful if people from every nation could meet and discuss everything from art to science without political overtones." I wonder if he ever printed that, but I felt it conveyed my attitude.

Angelo drove the four of us to the Grand Hotel de N'Gor which rises four stories in isolated white splendor on the ocean front, about a mile from the airport. On the patio, a stately Senegalese wearing a white shirt, red bolero, and huge ballooning black pants brought the limeades. This was pure ecstasy—warmth, a seat which did not vibrate, and the distant surf the only sound.

Mr. Mezzadri then returned to work. My crew and I agreed to meet again an hour later—time enough for me to shower, wash my hair and roll it up, put on my dress and tennis shoes, and cover the rollers with a white chiffon scarf. With some reluctance, but of necessity, I would appear in a foreign country as some women venture to the grocery store back home, but the warm air would dry my hair quickly.

From the taxis in front of the hotel, we selected one with a single red rose lying across the dashboard, giving a rakish touch to taxi and driver. We dropped Lee at the airport and continued toward what had impressed Earhart as a city of pink. I beheld a city of white as light-colored buildings dazzled in the brilliant sunlight. In front of the PAA building, Payne and Polhemus alighted. Polhemus, using French fairly fluently, instructed the driver to take me to the post office.

There I presented the letter from the postmaster of Dakar who had promised to assist on the flight covers. He had written a month before, happy we had chosen his country and city for the African cancellation.

The man behind the window read the letter, shook his head, and handed it to several other men, all of whom shook their heads. The letter was passed back through the bars. I had a sinking feeling.

"Does anyone here in the post office speak English," I asked the man.

He shrugged.

"May I help?" a friendly voice asked.

Turning, I saw it belonged to a man in his late twenties who wore a wide grin.

"My name is Manual. I speak English and five other languages."

"I have a letter from the postmaster here, but no one seems to know anything about our envelopes."

Manual read the letter. Returning to the window, he spoke rapidly in French. Then he said, "I'm sorry. The man here knows nothing about this and the postmaster is on holiday at the Ivory Coast."

"Guess it's up to me to get the envelopes stamped," I said dejectedly. "How is it you speak so many languages?"

"I'm a Portuguese sailor and I learned them by working on various lines and traveling all over the world."

I told him about the flight.

"You mean your husband would let you travel by yourself around the world?" Manual seemed surprised.

"I'm not by myself. There are three men with me."

At that he became more confused.

"My husband wanted me to go. Anyway, Earhart's husband didn't accompany her, only a navigator." I wonder what bizarre impression of female aviators was created in Manual's mind.

He offered to walk with me to the PAA building. As we crossed the wide boulevard, he asked, "Want some sugared popcorn?"

"Sugar on popcorn! We use salt! But I'll try some."

The popcorn, freshly made and sprinkled with finely ground crystals of sugar, was delicious. In fact, it was lunch, and, while trying not to appear too hungry, I did manage to eat my share.

In the PAA building Manual and I traced Payne and Polhemus to the American Air Office where they were waiting for some calls to be made by the man in charge.

"The clearances haven't arrived," Polhemus informed me. "We're trying to trace them now."

Before Manual left, he signed my black notebook which was rapidly filling with names and addresses of people who helped us. I promised to send him a post card from a further point en route.

The man hung up the phone. "No reports," he said. "And it will be impossible to get a call or cable through to the States until Monday morning. Everything goes through Paris and there they close Friday afternoon for the weekend."

"Monday morning!" I exclaimed. "We'll be behind schedule."

"We could fly the Lockheed and talk directly with Washington," Payne suggested.

Mr. McGinley from the United States Information Services had offered to help, but on the clearances no more could be done. However, he said his secretary would accompany me to the post office to purchase the stamps.

Jocylene spoke English fluently. Her long dark hair was

combed simply and she wore a chic shift. Fortunately, we had a driver from the agency as well as the car. Alioune, a tall thin Senegalese, spoke a little English and drove hurriedly toward the post office for it was ten minutes before closing time at five.

The shade had already been drawn at the stamp window, but Jocylene explained that we must buy the stamps this afternoon. Sheets of stamps were soon piled on the counter. My mouth felt dry even thinking of sticking them on the envelopes!

Then I told her about sending my slip and good shoes back to Michigan. At a department store we bought a slip. At the shoe store Jocylene said, "Put your foot beside mine. That way I can tell your approximate size. Hmmm. Your foot is a little longer. I wear a 36. You better ask for a 38."

"Size 38?"

"Of course that's in centimeters."

The clerk brought out a dozen pair of shoes. Most were fairly heavy looking and not comfortable. Finally, I tried a toeless pair with a medium heel and heelstrap. They fit reasonably well and were cool. How nice it was to instruct the clerk to wrap my tennis shoes; of course I preferred to wear the new shoes which looked decidedly better with the dress.

"The shoes are sixteen dollars American," Jocylene said. "Everything is expensive in Dakar. A man's shirt that you would pay seven or eight dollars for would cost twenty dollars here."

At the USIS agency office, I thanked Jocylene for helping immeasurably in obtaining the stamps and making the shopping enjoyable. Without her help, I would probably still be trying to get the shade raised at the post office. She instructed Alioune to take me to the hotel along the coastal drive which was lined with palms and stone terraces sloping gently toward the sandy beaches. Dakar reminded me of southern California with the semiarid land, the white buildings, the ocean, and the hills in the distance.

Polhemus and Payne were halfway through dinner in the hotel dining room. Joining them, I sank gratefully on the chair they offered.

"Hey, I like your shoes," commented Payne.

"About time you got rid of those tennis shoes," said Polhemus.

Payne continued, "We flew the Lockheed this afternoon. Lee had already attached the other antenna and drag cone when we stopped back at the airport. He's sleeping now. Really worn out from the work in Natal. We talked with AOPA. Permission has been granted for Bamako (Mali) and Kigali (Rwanda) but nothing has been heard from Bangui (Central African Republic), Kinshasa (Democratic Republic of the Congo) and Mogadiscio (Somalia). Also there are some uprisings in the Congo, and the State Department would be just as happy if we didn't go there."

"Guess that means no more Africa," I said.

Polhemus continued, "We asked AOPA to cable Barcelona, Rome, Ankara, and Tehran and advise Andrews when the clearances come. But, no problems are anticipated."

Payne added, "We've already sent clearance requests from here to Las Palmas in the Canary Islands and Lisbon, since we plan to leave Dakar Sunday morning."

"That sounds great—leaving and not knowing if we can complete the route as planned. But, we can't wait here or we'll never get to Howland on time."

During dinner the two men teased me about Everaldo and Manual, about how I always found a nice young man to help. I reminded them that Jocylene had also helped!

Dinner at the hotel that night was my first real meal in two days. Salad—crisp greens and tomatoes. Herring in sour cream—I finished the entire bowl. Steak—a shade past medium. Baked potatoes. Lime sherbet. Not only a "real meal," it was also delicious!

In my room I turned off the air-conditioner and opened the windows to the sea breeze. So, there was to be no more Africa— no Gao, a name which had intrigued me since I had first studied Earhart's itinerary; no Khartoum; and now not even Nairobi. Sometime I must return to Africa—to fly over the deserts with their drifting dunes, the jagged dry mountains and hills, the grasslands, and then finally to land at those cities I had been unable to see this time.

DAKAR

Saturday morning at the PAA office Angelo sent the alert cables detailing departure time for tomorrow and our schedule until arrival in Karachi. Then he drove Polhemus and me back to the hotel where a press conference had been arranged for 3:00 p.m.

At the appointed time, a dozen Senegalese were seated around tables on the veranda. An Australian, acting as interpreter, began the questions. There was always the problem of whom to look at during these sessions. The man posing the question looked at the interpreter. Then the Australian looked both at the man who had asked the question and at me while he translated. I answered in English. It was translated into French. What an intricate procedure for conversing! For two hours I answered the questions of these men in their flowing white robes. The UPI man, a native of Dakar, wrote in my notebook in French. "All my friendliness to Ann." I think all these men were worried about our old airplane.

We had been invited to a reception at the American Embassy. However, realizing that the flight covers must be stamped and cancelled this evening, I told the fellows I was going to the plane to get the envelopes.

The first problem at the airport was to get the boxes from the nose baggage compartment which is about eight feet above the ground. Inside the Lufthansa hangar a man was working in the loft.

"Do you have a ladder I could borrow?"

"I have no ladder," he replied in English, fortunately.

"What about using this boarding ramp?" I explained the problem.

"Yes, I'll help you roll it out as soon as I finish putting these things away."

Together, Peter Uber and I rolled the ramp to the Lockheed. Using a coin, I opened the two latches on the compartment. Then Peter climbed up and handed down the number of boxes I needed—two thousand envelopes. We put them on the ramp steps and rolled it to the terminal. After helping carry them inside, he left, telling me that we could use the ramp later if necessary.

Wanting no complications as a result of taking the boxes through customs and then to the hotel, I sat on the chairs on the airport side of the "customs gates" and began licking stamps. A half hour later only a small portion was affixed.

The custom's man was not busy, so I asked him, using sign language and gestures, if he would help. He nodded. We worked a few minutes and were joined by another man from customs. Sign language prevailed. Other employees in the terminal came. One of them spoke reasonably good English and I explained the flight and why the envelopes must be stamped and cancelled this evening. He told the story to the others.

What a sight we were—envelopes and stamps scattered around the waiting area. One elderly man insisted on putting the stamps on upside down and since he was so obviously happy to be helping, I said nothing, only cut down his supply of materials.

The envelopes could have been hand cancelled in a small post office in the terminal, but when the man saw the number to be done, he refused to stamp more than a few. He told me there was a cancelling machine at the airport postal station in the building adjacent to the terminal, so my helpers and I carried the envelopes there. The machine was operated by a hand crank, each revolution of the crank producing a cancelled envelope. A stack of 50 or so envelopes was put on the rack and as each batch came through I checked the envelopes, sending uncancelled ones through again. It was past eleven when the last envelope had been boxed. Half a dozen of the helpers and I carried the boxes to a jeep and then we towed the boarding ramp to the Lockheed. After the boxes had been put in the nose compartment, I felt the relief of realizing no more stamps to worry about until Karachi. Four days of freedom!

I thanked the people who had helped me and then phoned for a taxi.

At the hotel one of the clerks told me, "Your crew is waiting in the garden restaurant."

When I reached their table, they jumped up. "Where have you been?"

"At the airport getting the flight covers done."

"We were worried. We drove by the plane on the way to the reception. Figured you had gone to the embassy."

"I didn't get finished until after eleven. By then it was too late to attend the reception, so I just came back here."

"Why didn't you tell us!"

"I just forgot. I was busy and having a good time."

Knowing that we were to arise at 4:00 a.m., I cut that conversation short by remarking, "Don't you think it's time to retire?" Later, thinking of the concern my crew had shown that evening, and of how my brief disappearance had worried them, I realized what a closely knit family we had become.

LAS PALMAS
LISBON
ROME
ANKARA
TEHRAN

★ ★
★

IT WAS GOOD TO SLIP INTO CLEAN SLACKS AND JACKET
for the first time since leaving Detroit. The double charge for
same-day laundry service had been worth every penny. At
0700, Sunday, June 18, we began the flight north around Africa.
As we took off we dipped a wing to Polhemus who stood on the
airport below. He was jetting back to Ann Arbor for a week and
would rejoin us in Singapore.

On our left was the Atlantic. On our right, sandy plains and
hills with no sign of settlement broiled under the searing sun as
we flew up the African coast. Remembering how the oil temperatures had soared near the red line when we left Tucson, I
thought perhaps it was just as well we weren't subjecting the
engines to the African crossing.

The single runway at Port-Etienne, about 425 miles from
Dakar, stretched a silent simmering welcome 7000 feet below
our wings. Then, its refuge fell behind. With no airport in
range, had trouble developed with the plane, a wheels-up
landing on the shoreline would have been made.

I missed Polhemus's chatter on the interphone and also the
exercise of crawling back over the tanks to see his charts. We
felt that a member of our family had been lost; indeed we had
come to depend on each other to keep the flight running
smoothly.

Mr. Mezzadri had ordered every taste-tempting morsel—
from cold, tender thinly-sliced rolled roast beef to juicy apples—from the PAA kitchen for our food trays.

About noon, when we were an estimated 100 miles from the

Canary Islands, the 12,198 foot peak on Tenerife poked through the scattered clouds and was soon followed by the 6398 foot peak on Grand Canary Island. As we flew closer, other island peaks dotted the horizon.

Starting our letdown for the sea level landing, Payne said, "Las Palmas Approach. This is Lockheed Nan Seven Niner Two Three Seven." On all initial radio callups we prefixed the 79237 with Nan for the "N" preceding the number which meant the plane was under United States registry.

"Lockheed Two Three Seven. This is Las Palmas."

"Lockheed Two Three Seven descending for landing."

"Lockheed Two Three Seven. Are you civilian or military?"

"Civilian."

We continued toward the islands, continually losing altitude, the peaks becoming larger. Again the approach controller called, "Lockheed Two Three Seven. Are you a Navy airplane?"

"Negative, Civilian," Payne answered.

We "coasted on" Grand Canary Island and flew over the reddish mountain slopes, heading toward that wide concrete ribbon which could accommodate a four-engine jet. The man in the tower directed us to park about half a mile from the terminal. Maybe they didn't trust us yet!

The Shell truck arrived and we told the man our needs: fuel and a ride to the terminal.

In the airport manager's office, a high-ceilinged room with a three-bladed fan overhead, the credentials for us and the plane were examined. The men had thought the "N" in N79237 meant Navy and the USA at the end of the cable sent from Dakar requesting clearance to land meant U.S. Army. Confusing indeed! After the situation had been thoroughly explained, the atmosphere warmed considerably.

"What is the weight of your plane?" the manager asked.

"Ten thousand five hundred pounds," I replied.

"I need that in kilos."

Using Payne's conversion table, I changed the pounds to kilos.

The manager wrote the fee on a piece of paper, 243.35. How

could the landing fee be that much! Then he said it was $4.60 American. What a relief!

At 3:25 we left the islands behind and headed toward Lisbon. The scattered clouds dissipated as we flew north, and gradually the sun slipped over the horizon until only a thin red line remained. Behind the plane, the moon sent reflections glinting off the wings.

With the sun gone, it became cold in the cockpit at 7000 feet, so I zipped my jacket over my sweater and hoped for descent clearance soon. At 9:30 we were cleared to approach altitude, then to the radio beacon, and finally to Portello Airport. After thirteen flying hours we were 1800 miles north of Dakar. Polhemus would be nearing Ann Arbor.

After the plane was parked, pictures were taken. In spite of the warmer air, I was still shivering. Formalities took a few minutes in the terminal and then a stewardess interpreted for a reporter.

During the taxi ride to the hotel, I spent most of the time steadying myself on the bar which ran along the back of the front seat. My husband would never again have had complaints about anyone's driving if he could have ridden just once with this driver. Corners were taken on two wheels and people likely to get in his way received a raucous blast from the horn.

The hotel dining room was closed, but ham and cheese sandwiches were available at the bar. Yesterday, dinner had been nonexistent for me. This morning breakfast had been at five o'clock, lunch before noon, and tonight—sandwiches. Only when famished, and this evening I was, did I acquire more interest in food than in flight-related activities!

The next morning I changed my pesetas into American dollars and cashed another traveler's check into one dollar bills, figuring many items could be paid for this way and I would be spared the worry over foreign currency. In fact, U.S. dollars were popular and people almost seemed to prefer them.

Departing Lisbon at 9:30, we turned eastward on course across Spain. The stop at Barcelona had been eliminated because Rome was only 1178 miles, or about 8 flying hours away.

Control had cleared us to 10,000 feet where the flight suit

Don had put aboard at the last minute was added to my sweater and jacket. The entire heating system had been removed when the fuselage tanks had been installed. Clothing for a northern route and these altitudes had not been considered, as an equatorial route had been planned.

Lee, sitting in the navigator's seat, had wrapped our only blanket around him. Payne put on the jacket Don had insisted he take along and his leather flying boots kept his feet relatively warm. Cold in an airplane has a way of penetrating even the warmest clothing and my lightweight sweater and poplin jacket were far from that. Copies of two Lisbon newspapers had been purchased and after tearing out the articles about our flight, I wrapped my feet in the remaining pages.

When Polhemus called on the HF, he was worried about having enough fuel for the Pacific flights. He also suggested that Lee consider carrying our gear and flying commercially from Lae, New Guinea, to Honolulu. We postponed the decision until more data on fuel consumption was available, but the best way to add tankage was discussed. Since leaving the States we had been fueling with 100/130 octane instead of the 80/87 because fewer gallons per hour were used.

We crossed Sardinia and then in the distance saw the Italian coast. After making doubly sure the trailing antenna was in, we turned on final for Fumicini International, located on the coast an hour's drive from Rome. We had called PAA operations on the company frequency when still airborne and Mr. Setti Selmi greeted us. However, he had no cable from PAA authorizing him to assist us and we had no letter of introduction. He was sorry, but still, he would see what he could do.

A half hour later he returned. Everything had been cleared and he couldn't do enough for us. The fuel truck was hustled over. We were sped through formalities and soon he was opening the door of a taxi for the trip to the hotel in a coastal town twenty minutes away. Here I was flying around the world, yet we had passed well to the south of Paris and now we weren't even going to Rome! Perhaps on another trip these cities could be visited!

In the hotel dining room the waiter spoke enough English to be helpful. When the main course arrived so did a message that I was wanted on the telephone.

"How did you get to Rome so soon?" the reporter asked. "We were waiting for a cable from Barcelona."

"We decided not to stop there as it was only an eight hour flight here."

"Oh. I suppose now you're in the middle of dinner too."

"You're right, but go ahead with your questions."

He wanted to know everything—even why we now had only three aboard instead of four as he had read in the releases.

When the conversation had been completed, I returned to my lukewarm food, but the waiter said there was another call.

This time it was the AP man from Rome who hadn't been able to meet us. Finally a cold dinner was eaten.

The following morning we hitched a ride to the airport with a jetliner crew. Mr. Selmi had prepared **all** the papers for us and the airplane. Mr. Marincola, PAA operations man, took us to the weather briefing, and the flight plan was filed. Then, since it was raining, he escorted me to the Lockheed, holding a gigantic blue and white umbrella above my head.

The rain ceased over the Ionian Sea and we continued across Greece and the Aegean Sea, deep blue and dotted with islands. When we "coasted on" Turkey, the soil became reddish and the terrain mountainous with rock-strewn valleys.

Seven reporters from Ankara, including Midina, the first woman reporter encountered since leaving the United States, met us. She acted as interpreter. One of her first questions was, "Would you like to talk politics?"

"I'd rather talk about other things," I told her.

She asked many questions and translated the replies for newsmen. I asked her about Turkey. She was a delightful person and I would have liked to visit longer, but the customs men were waiting. There was no PAA facility here, so Celibi, a flying service, had been asked to assist us.

Pictures of B-25's were on the wall in the Celibi manager's office where we went for information on weather briefing and departure procedures. The manager said he had flown them many years ago in Colorado. I wondered in what capacity, but didn't inquire.

Abdullah, a Celibi employee, brought Turkish coffee in the traditional tiny cups on a tray suspended by three cords. He handed one cup to me, one to Payne, and the third to the manager. I drank the bittersweet liquid down to the finely ground coffee powder.

"Sometimes we tell fortunes with the grounds," Abdullah informed us.

The taxi driver who drove us the 27 kilometers to Ankara was not as reckless as the one in Lisbon, but he almost hit several people who darted into the street. Cows crossed the road as well as flocks of sheep. Fleece was hung on racks in many yards. Many horse-drawn carts shared the road with our taxi as we proceeded down the valley between the gently rolling hills.

After we registered at the hotel, Payne said he wanted to look for a Turkish horn. This was the first time the three of us had been able to do something like this together. We looked in several little shops, but the owners were more interested in selling us anything to get U.S. dollars than in helping us locate what we wanted. Then we tried one little shop near the hotel. Turan, the proprietor, knew a place where we might buy a horn, but by the time a taxi was found and we had driven there, the shop was closed. Back at the hotel I asked Turan where I could buy one of the diminutive cup and saucer sets.

"My friend whose store is only three blocks away, sells them. I can take you there."

Lee and Payne were more interested in dinner, so I alone went with Turan. At the china shop I bought a cranberry red cup and saucer which were carefully wrapped along with a package of Turkish coffee.

The next morning en route to the airport, we encountered soldiers stationed along the road at intervals, and the driver informed us that the President of Turkey and his wife were expected any moment, as they were flying out of the country on an official visit.

"You must get in the air as soon as possible or you'll have to wait until they have departed," he cautioned.

The men from Celibi helped us with the weather briefing and put a bag of food aboard. We started the engines and taxied past the band awaiting the arrival of the President.

At cruising altitude we ate the rolls, jam, and butter purchased from the cook at the hotel. I should have stopped there, but Celibi had given us some fruit in addition to the sandwiches we had requested. The apricots, larger than golfballs, had been picked at the just-ripe stage and the strawberries were huge, red, and juicy. I craved that fruit! Lee and Payne didn't eat any, but not having been bothered with intestinal problems so far, I ate most of it.

The mountains in eastern Turkey rise 13,000 feet and our assigned altitude was 14,000. Not only had we no oxygen and no heat, but also no choice. So we decided to follow the route as much as was necessary, flying through valleys when we could.

A hundred miles to the north was Mount Ararat, towering almost 17,000 feet. Along our course to the south, huge granite blocks, their peaks above us and topped with snow mantles, jutted skyward. Air currents from the rugged terrain below tossed the Lockheed in every direction and airspeed was reduced to 115 mph as it had been during the thunderstorms. These jolts did serve one useful purpose—they kept us awake in this oxygen-starved environment. The cold was so intense that I put my feet on top of the instrument panel where a tiny patch of sunlight made the difference between minimum comfort and freezing. Payne wore leather gloves. I kept one hand pocketed and wished I were small enough to curl up on top of the radio rack where it was warm.

The ADF could not be relied upon for navigation along this corridor because false signals were sometimes sent from the north to lure planes over territory which was off limits.

After crossing the mountains and descending to 11,000 feet where the outside air temperature was a warm fifty degrees, Payne pretended to fan himself as if he couldn't stand the heat!

COLONEL WILLIAM R. PAYNE, USAF.

Below were the desert and the arid mountains of Iran. At Tehran, the city in the middle of nowhere, a hot dry wind was gusting across the runway.

After landing, we started to turn toward the new terminal building which was on our right and where the PAA facility would be. However, the men in the tower instructed us to turn around and taxi to the old terminal on the other side of the field, even though we explained about PAA. In front of the old terminal, we shut down the engines. A policeman notified us that we were parked on the helicopter pad and would have to move 500 feet ahead, so we did.

Two men began talking with Lee who had been worried about the aluminum tabs which were on the front of the cowling at hinge points. They had bent slightly with the constant vibration and Lee thought they might crack. The men grinned and told Lee to give them one of the tabs. Fifteen minutes later they returned with new ones made of steel. Lee put them in place. He felt a superhuman responsibility for his Lockheed.

Joe Singh, a tall Indian and the PAA station manager, arrived wearing a white turban. "You should have been able to park by the PAA hangar at the new terminal," he told us. "I'll ride over with you and talk to the tower." We taxied to the new terminal. Then, after we had swung into position, the tower changed directions—we were in the right place but the plane must turn 180 degrees!

"I'm sorry about the delay," Joe told us. "The Shah arrived an hour ago. You can see the flower-covered ramp over there."

As we were telling a woman reporter from an English language Tehran paper about the two tabs the men had made, the photographer from her paper called. He had been taking pictures of the Shah and had not finished in time to meet us.

"Would you be available this evening?" the woman asked.

"We'll be at the Palace Hotel. He could come there."

Once in my hotel room, I felt the first faint suspicion I was not well. In fact, I vividly remembered those delicious apricots and strawberries! Nevertheless, I joined Lee and Bill in the hotel dining room. I was scarcely hungry, felt extremely tired, and for some reason was uncoordinated.

The potato soup needed salt and after Bill had salted his, I said, "Think I'll put some salt in mine too." Promptly I dropped the entire shaker in the bowl. Fortunately, the soup did not splash. The timing couldn't have been better in a well-rehearsed vaudeville act!

All I wanted to do was sleep and fell into bed, wondering if that queasy feeling inside was the legendary dysentery. It was!

At 10:00 p.m. the sharp jangle of the telephone awakened me. Who could that be? The desk clerk said, "There's a photographer here. He says he came by earlier and you weren't in." I had forgotten to leave word that we would be in the dining room!

"I'll be down in a few minutes," I told the clerk.

I dressed and went to the lobby where the photographer was setting up his equipment.

"I'm sorry I wasn't available earlier," I told him, explaining what had happened.

"Is OK, Miss," he said. "I take two quick shots and then I'm gone."

He did just that. Feeling the way I did, I was most anxious to return to my room, but as I walked past the desk clerk, he turned sparkling brown eyes on me and asked, "What is the best way to learn to fly? I want to be an airline pilot, but everything is so expensive here."

I told him about the Experimental Aircraft Association and showed him a picture of the airplane we had built.

Back in my room, I spent a short miserable night and was completely exhausted when the alarm jangled at 3:45. I skipped breakfast and walked in a dream world, mechanically following Lee and Payne.

After paying the taxi driver at the airport, I laid my wallet on top of my address notebook in my purse and walked up the terminal steps. Food must be purchased for the two men, But I could look at nothing but weak tea as a chaser for the dysentery medicine. When I tried to pay for the food, I missed my wallet. Again? I dug through the purse hopefully, but knew it must have slipped off the notebook. The loss was reported to Joe. Payne just shook his head. An announcement was made over the public address system, but no one turned in the wallet— no well-worn brown wallet with pictures, licenses, and credit cards.

Joe cabled PAA in New York and asked them to contact my husband so he could notify the credit card companies. On one point Don would cheer. For years he had wanted me to buy another wallet. Now I would have to!

Our food was paid for with borrowed money which would be added to our PAA bill, our thermos was filled with PAA approved water, and we climbed aboard the Lockheed.

At altitude, I lay on the air mattress Lee had inflated. It was chilly; so, wrapping myself in the thin cotton blanket, I shivered into a fitful sleep. When I woke, feeling miserable and cold, I wondered what I was doing halfway around the world, aching with the traveler's common malady and wanting to be anywhere except in an airplane 7000 feet over Iran.

KARACHI
NEW DELHI
CALCUTTA
BANGKOK

★ ★
★

AS I LANDED THE LOCKHEED on the wide runway at Maripur Airport on the outskirts of Karachi, a jeep bounced beside us, a cameraman hanging out the back.

Opening the door in front of the terminal after our frigid flight, we emerged into scorching heat—almost as if a giant oven had been turned on. A crowd surrounded us: Patrick Gonsalves from J. Walter Thompson Far Eastern Agency; Peter Riedel, the PAA Senior Maintenance Supervisor, and his wife Helen; other PAA personnel; representatives from Champion Spark Plug; airport officials; and news media people. We were at Karachi, back once again on the Earhart Trail.

Inside the air-conditioned terminal the health officer found our shot records in order. The interviews continued. A woman reporter wore the traditional long dress, but was very modern in her manner and questions.

"What has happened that was unusual?" I was asked. "Good or bad."

"I lost my wallet in Tehran this morning. My husband will probably kill me." Pencils jiggled as reporters filled their pads.

"Did you lose any money?"

"A couple dollars maybe."

Then question after question about the flight. One reporter stood out from the others not only because he was at least six foot three, but because he was most insistent. "I need two hours of your time tomorrow," he said.

"I'm not sure what our schedule will be," I told him.

"Well. I work for a major U.S. magazine and the UPI. There are lots of places for you to pose in Karachi and I definitely want a picture of you riding a camel."

That was my introduction to Daud. And I didn't feel like riding a camel!

"Here is my card," he said. "I'll give you a ring in the morning."

More pictures were wanted. I went to the plane—from air-conditioning to searing heat. A uniformed guard holding a rifle with saber was watching the plane. After the pictures had been taken, Lee, Bill, and I walked to the customs shed.

Lee decided to remain and begin the hundred-hour inspection. Bill and I waited for transportation to the KLM Midway House where airline crews stayed. When I told Payne I felt faint, he looked at me in mild disbelief—women pilots just were not supposed to be the fainting kind. However, I had eaten nothing since noon yesterday and had drunk only the dysentery medicine.

"I really think I'm going to faint," I told him again. Then I careened toward the sidewalk. When I regained consciousness, I was lying on a concrete bench in front of the terminal and Mrs. Riedel was sponging my face with a cold cloth. Never had I felt so tired before. Or so sick! All I wanted to do was sleep. Fortunately, all the reporters had departed.

At Midway House, Mohammed, a PAA employee, helped me to my room for I could barely walk. After he left, I collapsed on the bed.

It was still light outside, but it seemed days later when someone knocked on the double door leading to the courtyard. I opened the door. A smiling Pakistani stood there.

"I am Anayatulla Khan. Would you like something to make you feel better? Some soup? Some tea?"

"No thank you. I just want to sleep right now."

An hour later he was at the door with the same questions.

Again I said I just wanted to sleep. He bowed slightly and departed.

The third time he arrived, I was awake and ordered a soft drink. The next several hours were spent writing the letters and cards I had promised to send friends from the halfway point. Fortunately, Patrick Gonsalves had offered to get the Karachi flight covers stamped and cancelled.

The following morning about nine, Payne rapped on the door pane. "Are you awake in there?"

"Yes. Meet you in the lobby in ten minutes."

Then, another voice called through the door, this one vaguely familiar. "How are you feeling this morning?" asked Anayatulla. "I'll take your laundry. Have it back by four this afternoon."

"Just a minute. I'll hand it out the door."

When I entered the lobby a call was waiting from Patrick Gonsalves: Mrs. Shansi, an artist from J. Walter Thompson, would pick us up at ten o'clock. In the dining room Payne ate eggs, bacon, and toast. I drank tea. Lee had already gone to the airport to continue the hundred-hour inspection.

Driving with Mrs. Shansi, we passed carts with loads twice as high as the one or two small donkeys pulling them, often with the drivers sitting atop the bulging sacks. Stately camels, pulling wagons, plodded along disdainfully. Some wagons were drawn by horses and some by men. Flocks of sheep meandered along the well-traveled avenue. Cars were in the minority, and occasionally a bus chugged past, but small three-wheeled taxis darted by in unbelievable numbers. Mrs. Shansi dodged traffic skillfully—that headed in our direction as well as that moving in the opposite.

After Payne and I had met the JWT personnel, Mrs. Shansi, Patrick, Payne, and I ate in the dining room on the top floor of the International Palace Hotel. Such a smörgåsbord: cold roast duckling, molded salads, fresh fruits. And the desserts! I drank one cup of tea while the others feasted.

After lunch Mrs. Shansi took Payne and me shopping. The array of brass articles was incredible. I bought some mugs, candle holders, and a small gong. As we were paying for our purchases, the door opened.

"There you are," said Daud, a smile covering his face. "At last I've found you. Why didn't you call me this morning? I called you and left a message."

"We had too many things to do and I really don't feel like riding a camel today."

"Well, now that I'm here, I'll just follow you in my car until you have some time for me."

Mrs. Shansi drove us to a shoe store. Daud followed. By this time it had been proposed by Daud and accepted by Mrs. Shansi and Payne that not only should I ride the camel but do it in a Pakistani outfit. Mrs. Shansi called the office and spoke with Mr. Bokhari, the president.

His sister Zehra would be expecting us and have a suitable outfit ready. Daud trailed us to her house. Every time Payne and I turned to see if he was behind us, he waved and honked.

Zehra Bokhari, an extremely attractive girl, told me she wanted to become an airline stewardess, but was quite nervous about the approaching interview. After I changed into her baggy white pants and a hip-length floral tunic, she wound a violet print scarf around my shoulders. The attire was surprisingly cool.

At the American Consulate, Mr. Gibson handed me a cable from Andrews and said he had been puzzled about the contents. We had not been able to contact Andrews or Liberty Airways en route from Tehran, but they had not forgotten us. No wonder Mr. Gibson had had difficulty—many references were to Rapid Rocket and upper sideband!

"When Earhart was here in 1937," he continued, "Karachi was a fishing village of 300,000. Food is marketed much as it was thirty years ago, but now we have three million people and problems with housing and schools."

"There seem to be many things which probably haven't changed in thirty years," I replied. "The donkey carts. The camels. But in terms of flying, jets land here from all parts of the world."

Mr. Gibson said they had a file on Earhart, but it would have to be found in past records and we didn't have time to wait. When Mrs. Shansi said she had to leave to fix dinner for

KARACHI: Talking with Pakistani girls on the beach.

her children, Daud beamed. "Now you can ride a camel. It is only a short distance to the beach."

Payne and I shrugged. Perhaps this was the only way to appease Daud. Certainly I didn't relish riding a camel at midnight!

Daud stopped his car and ran toward some girls walking to the beach. He could be charming when he wanted and soon I was talking with them while he took pictures. They were studying mathematics and economics and no veils hid their faces. Each one signed my notebook.

At the end of the road was a low stone wall and below it, the beach. When we stopped, a group of camel drivers, each leading a huge dun-colored beast, descended upon us—all shouting praise of their animals. Daud selected one and the other owners departed, grumbling.

I had ridden horses and steers, but never a camel. The

KARACHI: Camel ride.

driver commanded the aloof animal to kneel, and after repeated urgings, the huge beast finally put his knees on the sand, turned his head, and nibbled the saddle. I decided to keep my knees well back. In fact, since the saddle was tandem, I would sit in the rear seat!

The driver whacked the saddle and a small sandstorm erupted. I shuddered, thinking of the borrowed clothing that must be returned that evening.

"Up you go," said Daud, helping me aboard and then stepping back. Payne was enjoying my plight, and in fact, had his camera ready.

Suddenly, the back end of the camel rose. I grabbed for the saddle. Another lurch and the front end followed.

"Trot back and forth," commanded Daud, getting his camera ready.

The driver led the camel.

"No good," said Daud. "You have to ride it alone."

The driver relinquished the reins. I had visions of a charging camel carrying me down the beach until I fell off intentionally to keep from being abducted into the next country. I gripped the saddle with my knees and shook the reins. The camel turned his head and stared at me. I stared back. Clearly, I had to show him who was boss. I kicked him in the ribs. He moved forward a couple of steps and stopped. Payne laughed. Daud was waving his camera impatiently. "Trot by me so I can take a picture," he said.

I thought walking the camel was fast enough.

"No. We need action," said Daud.

Yelling at the camel, I administered a sharp jab in its ribs. The camel trotted, a lumbering seesawing gait. I held the reins firmly and kept him turning so he couldn't build up speed. Back and forth we trotted, Daud shouting instructions. "Head up. Smile. Now once more."

Payne had finished his roll of film and was still laughing. I had begun to feel miserable inside again! Then, mounted on my camel, I suddenly felt something else—the determination to enjoy the ride in spite of the dysentery, for never again might I ride a camel in Karachi.

"Hey, Daud," I hollered. "Let's get Payne up here too."

Daud grinned. "All right. In the front saddle he goes. Watch the camel's teeth."

The camel knelt again, an act only slightly less spectacular than his getting up, and Payne climbed aboard. Around we trotted with Daud calling encouragements. The camel driver probably wondered just what was going on.

When I was once again on the solid earth, I felt very much a part of that beach, and, obviously, from the amount of sand I had collected, the beach was very much a part of me.

The drive back to Midway House was almost wilder than riding the camel. Although Daud drove skillfully, he made the Lisbon driver seem tame. Daud would have made quite a pilot, as all turns were banked and no stop signs heeded—there are none in the sky! Wise people stayed out of his way. Several times he jammed the brakes, the car skidded, and we narrowly missed veiled women who looked neither right nor left as they darted into the street. Perhaps they thought their veils would protect them.

When I returned the clothing to Zehra, I apologized for the sand, but she just laughed.

At Midway House, more newsmen were waiting. In fact, they had been there since four o'clock. It was now after five and Bill, Lee, and I were eating dinner with Mr. Bokhari at six.

The reporters were eager to interview me. I was eager to shower and get dressed for dinner. This was explained and the men reluctantly agreed that ten minutes be allowed for this.

In my room I locked the door. No sooner had I stepped from the shower than someone knocked and a note was slipped under the door.

> Mrs. Ann.
> I want a separate meeting. It would be better to sit in your room because I think my photographer would be able to snapp a different poses.
>
> Thanks.
>
> Newsman.

They had barely given me five minutes. This was indeed the jet age! Just then Anayatulla banged on the door and shouted, "Your laundry is here." I jumped into my dress, thankful not to have to spend time choosing what to wear and opened the door. I paid him for the laundry. Behind him were the newsmen and his photographer.

"Two more minutes," I told them. Shoes. Some lipstick. My single strand of beads. I was ready.

The two men came in the room. The interview was short for I still had to talk with the others in the lobby. The photographer took some pictures. They promised to send several copies of the newspaper. (They kept that promise, but I could not read one word of what had been written.)

As I finished talking with the newsmen in the lobby, the car arrived to take us to the Sind Club where Mr. Bokhari was waiting. The atmosphere was sedate, the food served with a flourish, and my hamburger pattie and soup were delicious. It was good to be eating again!

The next morning at the airport, Payne turned in our flight plan. Then he was informed that it would have to be redone on Pakistani forms. Bill was perturbed by this delay, as his tightly pursed lips and the absence of jovial comments made clear to me.

At customs, one of the inspectors was going through the entire contents of a trunk owned by a glowering man. When we came with our luggage, the inspector glanced briefly at our forms, signed them, and waved us through. I didn't dare to look at the man whose trunk was undergoing such a thorough inspection.

Daud arrived, carrying a small envelope and several newspapers. "You see," he said, "I am not as bad as you thought. Here are the things I promised you."

In the envelope were pictures of various sizes, copies of what he had taken yesterday.

"Film paper is very expensive here so we hoard it. My scissors save money for me. A roll of 35mm color film costs $10.00."

Airborne, we tried to contact Andrews and Liberty Airways on the frequencies suggested in the cable, but neither responded. It was day here and night there so when our higher frequencies reached the darkness they penetrated the thinner ionized layer instead of being reflected. Lower frequencies would have been absorbed by the thicker ionized layers present during daylight before reaching the area of darkness. Payne contacted another station in the HF network and the men there relayed our message to Andrews.

The direct route to New Delhi was shorter, but the airways did not cross the Thar Desert. Instead our flight path went past Hyderabad to the CHOR radio beacon 171 miles east of Karachi, then to Udaipur and from there northeast to New Delhi.

The Indus River was a welcome break in the dun-colored

landscape with its arid rocks and sand, which impressed me as a terrain hostile to living creatures unless they were especially adapted to its rigors.

Later the land was dotted with numerous "small villages" designated likewise on the map. Had they been there thirty years ago? Or had Earhart flown over even more desolate territory? I estimated roughly that each village consisted of twenty to one hundred buildings of various sizes. Fields, some green, were laid out around the boundary. Dirt roads connected these settlements, and in spite of the haze which reduced our visibility, we always had several of these villages in sight.

About a hundred miles east of Udaipur, a black mountain, Guru Sikhar, poked its peak above the sea of scattered clouds. From the plain it rose 5650 feet above sea level across several miles. This one peak could have been a miniature mountain range stretching from northeast to southwest for fifteen miles.

When we were near enough and had been instructed to do so, we called the tower at Palam Airport.

"Lockheed November Seven Niner Two Three Seven. Proceed to the beacon," the man said rapidly.

We descended from our cool 7000 feet to the heat of the New Delhi area. At the beacon Payne radioed again. This time the man rattled so fast that only a few words could be caught. "Another plane. . . ." Payne asked the man to "Say again." The jargon was unintelligible. Although it was English the man in the tower had spoken, we certainly could not understand it.

"Understand cleared for landing," Payne said.

Since the reply didn't sound too excited, we flew inbound keeping a lookout for other traffic.

"Lockheed Two Three Seven. . . ." again the garbled rush of words.

We continued the approach, landed, and taxied to the terminal. "Taxi east. . . ." said the man in the tower. We asked him to repeat. I would have given this man the highest rating for rudeness of any tower operator in the world. Obviously, he realized we could not understand him. Then why didn't he speak slower? When we came within a thousand feet of the terminal, the voice became more agitated, but still we could not understand.

"Want us to stop here?" Payne asked.

"Yes!" the man practically shouted. "Stop there."

We shut down the engines. What now? The heat of the ramp steamed upward. We waited. Finally, the blue and white PAA van approached. The men inside were friendly. We told them about the tower operator and they assured us it was all right to park the Lockheed where it was—in the middle of a vast concrete ramp.

En route, we had transferred only enough fuel to make New Delhi so no extra time would be taken filling the fuselage tanks for the flight to Calcutta.

Payne and I rode to the terminal and Lee stayed to fuel the plane.

"We have a package for you," the PAA man said. "But it is in customs downtown. We can take you there."

The package contained additional film and my shoes, but there was no time for a trip downtown.

"It might be easier for you to get it in Bangkok where customs are not so strict," a PAA man suggested.

I told him to ship it via PAA to Bangkok.

"I'll do that today," he said, "and it should arrive before you do tomorrow evening. Here is a cable for you."

The message was from the Governor of Kansas, Earhart's home state. How strange to receive this in the middle of India, but I was becoming accustomed to the unexpected.

The PAA man said that some airplane builders and the Press had expected us two days earlier. In fact, PAA had ordered a crew to meet us and we hadn't arrived. Their flights came in several times a week and help was paid for the time they were needed. We were billed for the first "meeting."

Having been on the ground slightly more than an hour, we started the engines with no delay, as monsoons were reported between New Delhi and Calcutta, 810 miles east, and we did not want to dodge them in darkness. With the comparatively light load of fuel, the Lockheed climbed quickly. Ahead were faint traces of clouds which were the forecast storms. For once the headwind was less than anticipated and groundspeed averaged 143 mph. Fortunately, the storms were to the south of our course—not so far south, however, that we missed the sunset turning the cloud formation into golden-red towers of an ancient city.

We landed at Dum Dum Airport an hour after sunset. PAA personnel made us feel at home immediately. Mr. Ganguly, the Senior Maintenance Supervisor, took us through customs, where, after we were introduced, a handshake completed our luggage inspection. Although Lee and Payne kept joking that customs were so easily passed because of me, I gave full credit to PAA's efficiency and assistance!

We did, however, have to fill out extra general-declaration forms for entry into the country and list foreign currency, Indian currency, watches, cameras, valuable gems, dangerous drugs, arms and ammunition, and even fountain pens. Another form called for the amount of fuel on board the Lockheed upon landing and the amount which would be taken on.

Because of the darkness in the area where the plane was being fueled, Lee spilled some oil on his clothing. This was a problem as clothes were so limited. With typical good humor, he wiped it off and said he would wash the spots with soap at the hotel.

The terminal was crowded with people on benches waiting for and filling out the endless forms required for traveling. The health officer took more of our time. After filling out a form which asked our purpose for staying in the country, I handed the three passports to the man in charge of immigration. Finally, immunization records and passports were returned.

During the time we had been waiting, I talked with the airport correspondent from the "Statesman" and a reporter from a Calcutta newspaper printed in Hindi.

Mr. Ganguly drove us to the Grand Hotel. He kept his headlights off, insisting he could see better this way, and flicked them on only when he saw oncoming traffic and wanted to be sure they saw him. I felt we were hurtling through a dark subway tunnel.

The narrow streets seethed with people, and the houses, wooden shacks with fronts that were rolled up or down depending on the degree of "privacy" desired, nestled in unending rows. Small lanterns flickered, illuminating people sitting on front steps or on chairs on the sidewalks. On street corner after street corner hundreds of people without homes had spread their sleeping mats, placing their possessions beside them.

At the entrance of the Grand Hotel was a mass of Indians, all holding out their hands, the children with distended bellies signifying malnutrition. Mr. Ganguly cleared a path for us through this wall of human misery. It was here, in the cities, that poverty and hunger seemed worst. It was hard to imagine a similar condition in the villages where food was grown nearby.

Not being dressed for dinner, we ate on the inside patio. No Coke was available, so we drank some lemon soda, and joked about a rumor we had heard about local pop bringing on dysentery. There was nothing else to drink except hot tea and we wanted something cool. The pop was cold. Iced tea would have been welcomed, but ice was not to be trusted.

Our waiter informed us of a newsman who wanted to talk with us. There was a fourth chair at the table so Santosh Basak, the East India correspondent for the AP, sat with us.

Santosh was a pleasant dinner companion and took in good grace our teasing complaints about never being allowed to eat without interruptions.

Lee told him Calcutta had not changed, except for more people, since he had been stationed there during World War II.

The Grand Hotel was a relic of the English and was now past its glory. It had an air of somewhat scarred elegance, to which the furniture, especially, contributed. A prime example was the valise rack in my room, with its scratches attesting indisputably to the thousands of suitcases which had been flung upon it.

The huge marble-floored room and additional dressing and lavatory areas had fifteen-foot ceilings which gave one the impression of being in a castle. Though there were two double beds the room seemed spacious. A pair of slip bolts locked the door and I used both.

Payne called and said he had ordered breakfast to be sent

to each of our rooms shortly past five. Maybe this was the way to save time and still eat. Often we had missed breakfast completely.

The eleven hours flying plus the formalities and interviews left me exhausted but still unreconciled to missing anything. Perhaps that was the trouble! I wanted to take in everything and needed to be three people to do so. It was easy to appreciate how tired Amelia must have been during her flight with no one to share her responsibility for the plane.

It was midnight before I fell asleep. At five the next morning the telephone rang. I dressed hurriedly. At 5:20 breakfast arrived. My copilot had observed well what I liked for this meal: scrambled eggs, toast, and tea. Such a necessary luxury, this breakfast "almost" in bed!

On the drive to the airport, Mr. Ganguly pointed out the showers—pipes along the street. Some people were still asleep on the corners. Cattle, looking better cared for than people, meandered in the streets. Rickshaws were plentiful, but I, with two strong legs, would have felt guilty riding in one. Indeed, both driver and passenger might be better off if they changed places.

At the airport, Payne and Mr. Ganguly went to flight operations and obtained a weather briefing. Then came customs, immigration, and health. Lee checked the plane and PAA mechanics watched as he tightened screws on the cowlings. Payne returned to get more customs forms from our folder and muttered something about the red tape being formidable. He wore a tense angry look on his face—the same as he had in Karachi.

When Payne returned we slipped into our over-water harnesses, to which parachutes could be attached quickly. Our route lay across the Bay of Bengal and then over Burma. An hour after our intended departure time the wheels left the runway. Lee hadn't had time to wash the windshield, so we flew the Lockheed underneath the edge of a rainstorm. When the plane emerged, the windshield was clean. We laughed. As tired as we were, the labor saved counted as a double reprieve.

We flew southeast, over the many inland arms of the Bay of

CALCUTTA: Mechanics from PAA watch Lee make some adjustments.

Bengal, really the mouths of rivers, then over a corner of East Pakistan, and subsequently over open water. As if some magic wand had swept a way clear for us, the monsoons were on our right and left while our course remained clear except for small storms and billowing clouds. These miniature storm systems were complete even to the rainbows which followed us, darting across the whiteness and mists of the backsides.

The verdant lushness of the Burmese mountains was visible through breaks in the clouds to our left. We "coasted on" Burma near Andrew Bay, first flying over the mountains we had seen from offshore and then over the lowlands with their many rivers and few towns. Over Rangoon we informed the air traffic controller that we desired to proceed direct to Bangkok. However, I did take a picture of the huge Shwe Dagon Pagoda between the scattered clouds.

We continued over the Gulf of Martaban, over the Bilaui Tauno Range and the swampy plain where Bangkok lies.

Reporting north of the airport, we were cleared to land after a hospital airplane. This being an R & R (rest and recreation) city for servicemen in Viet Nam, the army-colored planes were numerous. Still, it was hard to imagine that a war was being fought such a short distance away.

PAA personnel met us, their blue and white van buzzing to our parking spot. One of the men stared at the plane and finally asked, "Where are the other two engines? I thought Electras had four engines."

"This was the first Electra," I explained. The word Electra must have appeared on the flight plan.

My first task was to retrieve the package from customs. It took twenty minutes to find someone who knew where the package was in the shed and more time to locate the package and sign the forms. Finally, the package was opened to confirm what had been listed on the sheets. Then it was resealed. It was to be put aboard the plane and not be opened until we were airborne the next day. Possibly the twenty reels of 16mm film and the dozen rolls of still film worried them.

Inside the terminal we cashed some checks into local currency, noting carefully how many Thai units equaled one U.S. dollar. Each day we dealt with a different currency!

Bangkok was completely different from Calcutta. The streets were clean, the buildings newer, and the shops displayed an interesting array of every conceivable item. The rickshaw-type carts were bicycle propelled. More cars were seen on the streets.

The Siam Inter-Continental Hotel was 90 percent completed. It boasted furnishings as modern as in Miami and plugs with three different voltages. The menu was so varied that a traveler from any country would have felt at home.

The next morning I took a short walk before breakfast. The Thai people seemed busy, industrious, and friendly. There was little begging and the residents streamed toward their jobs in cars, busses, and on foot.

At breakfast, Payne mentioned he didn't feel particularly well. Lee had come down with dysentery and I wasn't feeling my best either. At the airport it was again apparent that I did indeed have dysentery. We could not delay the flight, so the medicine was shared.

Airborne, no one felt well. So far, the "Blue Room" had not been used because the first one doing so had to empty the container. Today no one argued!

This second bout with dysentery left me with almost no energy. Lee and Payne joked about the soda pop in Calcutta! All of us had drunk it, and the timing was about right. Feeling this weak was unlike me, and I found it hard to accept. I spent some time resting on the air mattress. The tailwinds zoomed our groundspeed to 152 mph, pushing us down the eastern coast of the Malay Peninsula until we saw the green slope with huge white letters spelling SINGAPORE. Beside it was the airport. Polhemus would be waiting and once again it would be four people and one old airplane against the elements.

SINGAPORE
DJKHARTA
KUPANG
DARWIN

★
　★
★

THE OPENING LINE IN A LETTER from Mr. Gonzalves, PAA Airport Manager, was "Selamat Datang Kawan," which meant "Welcome to you, my friend."

David Adcock, PAA Customer Service Manager, told us Polhemus had arrived about two hours ago and was waiting at the hotel. The feats so common to this jet age will never cease, I think, to impress me. The Lockheed had taken seven flying days to get from Dakar to Singapore. Polhemus had jetted from Dakar, spent almost a week with his company and then his flight to Singapore had taken less than 24 hours.

Lee had been waiting for me to finish talking with David. Then he said, "Ann, this is Roy Norris. His father met Earhart when she landed in Singapore."

"That's right," affirmed Roy. "She landed at Seletar Air Base, a grass field and the RAF station. My father was a storekeeper on the station and was especially proud of a picture taken of him and Amelia beside her Electra. He was killed in an accident seven years ago."

"I'm sorry to hear that. Do you still have that picture? I'd like to see it."

"I might be able to find it, but don't count on it. If I do, I'll bring it to the airport tomorrow."

Roy, Senior Maintenance Supervisor with PAA, helped Lee fuel the plane and put on the elevator locks. The nozzle for the fueling hose was too large, so Robert J. Kennedy, the Shell representative, arranged for Lee to use a smaller one. Robert

SINGAPORE: Roy Norris, whose father met and helped Amelia Earhart in 1939 when she landed at Singapore, helps Lee. Robert Kennedy locates and exhibits a smaller nozzle for fueling.

was the kind of person who knew where to purchase anything. When with him I had the impression the city was a roadmap on his palm, his mind a guidebook to Singapore. The entire group here was young and energetic and we had immediately sensed that they wanted to make our short stay a pleasant one. A more lively and alert bunch we had never met, nor one that seemed to enjoy their jobs so much. As we were leaving for the hotel, David said, "You can't get rid of us. We'll meet you at the hotel in an hour for a beer!"

In my hotel room was a plate of fruit, wrapped in golden cellophane, compliments of George Milner, the manager. The package was too beautiful to open, but the fruit must be shared!

Downstairs in the cocktail lounge, I found my crew and David Adcock. Polhemus stood up. "Gee, you're looking great," he said and planted a kiss on my cheek. "From Don," he added.

"Yeah," I replied. He hadn't changed. The same grin. The same spirit. It was great to have him aboard again!

David and Polhemus drank beer, the rest of us a soft drink. Just to relax a few moments was heavenly.

"We still haven't received a clearance from Indonesia," Polhemus said. "David is going to try to get one through their facilities in Djkharta. PAA has a flight going in there once a week."

"No clearance yet! What do we do if we don't get one?"

"Try to fly via Borneo and hope for the best," said Polhemus. "By the way, I think by careful planning we won't need those extra fuel tanks."

That was good news. But, one problem solved, there were always others to take its place.

Dinner for me was consommé and tea. Polhemus ate everything on his plate and commented that drinking beer had kept him free from dysentery. Lee, Payne, and I scoffed. Probably Polhemus had a natural immunity to germs or maybe that second vaccination had a beneficial side effect!

My phone rang at 5:45 the next morning. A cable from Andrews had been relayed through the PAA facility in Singapore. We were to contact the American Consulate General here before departing for Djkharta.

At half-past nine a long-distance call came through from CKLW in Detroit. We were halfway around the world according to time zones, as it was 9:30 p.m. there.

Three notes had been slid underneath the door, two from news media people, and one saying that a press conference had been arranged for half-past eleven at the hotel.

At ten o'clock Robert Kennedy drove Payne and me to visit the American Consulate General. The building was attractive, but the windows looked strange.

"Remember the riots and stone throwing here? This was the building. That's cellophane on the front windows. The rioters were really a small group, just looking for trouble. We here laughed at them for they were ineffective, but abroad the story was blown up out of proportion in the newspapers and on television. It was a far smaller crowd than apparently filled the television screens."

However, many of the items in the newspapers in the countries we visited were of the sensational type. Upon returning to the States, however, I would cut in half the reported importance of incidents of this type—especially the size of the crowds that threw rocks.

In John Sullivan's office, we explained our need for a clearance. Immediately, he sent a cable to Indonesia, and said we would be notified at the hotel when the reply was received.

Since Payne, Lee, and I were still feeling the effects of dysentery, Robert took us to a drugstore which charged "honest rates" and recommended we purchase Entero Vioform. I bought three containers.

As we drove around the city, Robert said, "We are proud of Singapore. New apartments and hotels are being constructed. The export and import business is growing. It is a new country in many respects and will become even better."

At the hotel the press people were waiting. While I was talking with them, the assistant hotel manager brought me an exotically delicious fresh fruit punch called a "welcome drink."

David Wilson, talks correspondent with the ABC (Australian Broadcasting Commission), wanted to tape an interview, so he joined Robert, Payne, and me for lunch. I ordered poached eggs and then swallowed two of the pills now dubbed Kennedy's Remedy.

Lee was installing the shoulder harnesses—long automobile seat belts purchased this morning. In the event of ditching, pilot and copilot would not be flung against the instrument panel. Polhemus was getting the Singapore flight covers stamped and cancelled.

The clearance arrived. We were booked as a special PAA flight departing Singapore at 4:00 p.m., remaining overnight in Dikharta, and stopping for fuel at Kupang on the island of Timor en route to Australia tomorrow.

At the airport David asked me to do him a favor. His

secretary was out for the day and wanted me to sign her autograph book. Now this was not just an ordinary book, David told me, for it contained something not seen often, the autograph of Charles A. Lindbergh who had signed it during one of his exploratory flights. The secretary wanted my signature on the opposite page.

Too soon our luggage was stowed and we were waving to David, Roy, and Robert. As we tucked the wheels up and headed south, I like to think that it was Roy Norris who watched until our silver wings were a speck in the distant blue, as his father might have done with another Lockheed 10 thirty years ago.

In March a letter and a call had been received from Raymond King, a Representative in the Kansas Legislature, inviting us to come to Newton, Kansas, on our way to California. He and Arnold Lewis, a reporter from the Wichita Eagle, had flown to Detroit to see us off. Earhart had been born in Atchison, Kansas, which explained the invitation to visit that state. Since we could not accept the invitation then, plans now called for us to stop there on the return flight from California to Detroit.

As we flew south toward Djkharta, Andrews informed us that Don was on the phone wanting to know if we could arrive at Newton on Sunday, July 9. I told him it was feasible if we encountered no delays. Also, he said that Saline, Michigan, where we lived, was planning a parade and welcoming festivities for July 15, the Saturday following our return.

The afternoon sun and the monsoon clouds on our left produced triple rainbows, the colors blending into the mists. Later, the reddish gold clouds of sunset reflected on our silver wing.

It was dark when we were cleared for a straight-in approach over the radio beacon north of Djkharta. Because the lower switches were not well lighted, the one for the left landing light had a handle twice as long as the one for the right. I flicked both of them up. Two beams penetrated the darkness, illuminating the runway ahead.

After parking, we waited several minutes, but no one came over. Then I took passports, immunization records, and the plane's papers and walked across the ramp to a lighted office. Inside, ten men looked at me with expressionless faces. Our flight was posted on the blackboard. The men here were not connected with PAA, but they were obviously in charge of operations on the airport. I introduced myself to one of them who asked when we planned on leaving in the morning. Since we had to fly to Darwin with an intermediate stop at Kupang, where there were no runway lights, we wanted an early start.

"Eight o'clock," I told him.

"Nine will be better," he replied in a way so that further discussion would be useless. "Take the passports and health records to the terminal next door."

Leaving that office, I felt eyes burning holes in my back. Inside the terminal were rows of wooden benches. The customs officials were at one side, patiently checking several bags. One of them told me to bring the suitcases through when we left for the city and indicated I should take the shot records and passports to another office.

In that office, a man wearing a uniform was sitting behind a desk. He nodded curtly. I was determined to be pleasant and patient. First he asked to see the papers for the crew, and I gave them to him, one set at a time, somehow not wanting him to have all of them at once. In fact, when he had finished looking at them, he said, "Perhaps you would like us to keep them for you tonight."

"No thank you," I replied. "I can just put them in my purse." Would they have been returned in time for a morning departure?

I asked him where hotel rooms might be available. He wrote a number on a piece of paper and said I could use his phone. This was the first gesture of anything resembling friendliness encountered since landing.

The line was busy. Waiting to try again, I said, "You probably work long hours."

The man relaxed slightly, smiled ruefully, and said they

worked every day at least twelve hours and sometimes more. No wonder he had seemed so matter of fact, so resigned; and probably the pay was not the best either.

I dialed the number again. This time someone answered but said no rooms were available.

"Is there some other hotel we could call?"

The man wrote another number. "Try this one," he said. "It's the only other hotel that would be comfortable."

No rooms were available there. I had visions of us flipping coins to see who got the air mattress and who the blanket. Maybe those parachutes were softer than imagined.

I told the man I would see him in the morning to sign the papers for plane and crew.

At the Lockheed my crew was talking with the PAA representative who said he had reserved four rooms at the Hotel Indonesia, the first hotel I had called. After Lee refueled the plane, the man from PAA drove us to the hotel. It was always difficult to obtain an impression of a city, especially at night, from the brief glimpses snatched while en route to our sleeping quarters. After driving through streets resembling a slightly less crowded Calcutta, we turned onto a boulevard. I was prepared in no way for the hotel I saw, which would have been appropriate in any large city in the United States. Modern in both architecture and lighting effects, it looked almost incongruous in comparison with the surrounding buildings.

At the desk, the PAA man talked with the clerk who then frowned.

No rooms were available! That seemed odd as two floors had unlighted windows. Were the rooms not ready for occupancy or just empty? Or weren't we welcome at the hotel?

We mentioned the apparently empty rooms to the clerk who looked a little flustered. Then the manager appeared and assured us no reservations had been received. His manner was so high handed, so aloof, that I began not caring whether we ever got a room here. He said there were no rooms and left us. We stayed by the counter. The clerk, embarrassed by our presence, would not look our way. Finally he said, "I have a room for four for $60." By that time I was ready to sleep in the bathtub—but $60!

We said that was too much. Had they figured we would accept immediately? The clerk then phoned what he called the Press Club, a small hotel two blocks behind the Hotel Indonesia. Four rooms were available at $2.50 each. The PAA man drove us there and we checked in. The hotel was filthy. I don't think the lavatory and shower area had been cleaned in five years. The restrooms were communal and I felt that women probably didn't stay at this hotel very often.

Walking back to the coffee shop at the Hotel Indonesia after we changed clothes, we noted thousands of people milling around on the hotel grounds. The menu could have been copied from a small restaurant back home. We ordered hamburger dinners. I took two of Kennedy's Remedy and passed the container to Payne and Lee. Polhemus was still relying on beer.

Since I did not want to use the restroom at the Press Club, Polhemus and I walked to the lobby area of the Hotel Indonesia, used the restroom facilities, and then returned to our hotel.

My room contained two beds with thin mattresses, each covered by a slightly used gray sheet. Across one bed lay a clean towel. In a corner of the room was a lopsided wooden wardrobe, and a table lamp threw its yellow shadow against the peeling wall.

Outside in the courtyard, the nightly program had begun. Over a loudspeaker blared the wailing singsong, the wildly weird modal chanting of what someone said was a political puppet show. Indeed, I felt the people were more the puppets in this country. This show, we had been told, ran until it began to get light. How did these people get any sleep, much less accomplish anything the following day? Another time, I might have been more intrigued with the political-musical happening, but tonight I was too tired. After jamming chairs in front of the two doors, I put on my bathrobe, covered myself with the towel, lay gingerly on the sheet, and in spite of the cacophony outside, fell asleep immediately.

The next morning the fellows looked tired. Lee had battled mosquitoes all night and had used the mattress of the second bed for a blanket. The two Bills reported similar situations.

Thus, with no mosquitoes, and being able to sleep through the noise, I had spent perhaps the most restful night of all.

After paying the hotel bill in local currency and stopping for a quick breakfast at the coffee shop, we loaded luggage and ourselves into a small taxi which had been ordered the night before.

Customs went quickly since everything except clothing had been left in the plane. When Polhemus and I were at Immigration, a man came with a paper for me to sign for the landing fee. I told him that PAA would handle the payment and to give them the papers.

At the Lockheed, Lee was angry, but amused at the irony of the situation. Someone had seen gasoline dripping from the fuel-overflow pipe under the wing—a normal occurrence as the fuel expanded from the sun's heat—and had inserted a rag to stop the flow. As a result, fuel had overflowed at the filler neck and run on the outside of the tank into the wheel well and along the spar. Because the gear was electric and any small spark could have ignited the mixture, we waited until the gasoline evaporated. Somebody had tried to help!

Nine o'clock! Polhemus was worried about reaching Kupang before sunset as there were headwinds. Finally, the clearance came and we taxied to the active runway, passing a Russian jet bomber on the ramp and what appeared to be a class surrounding it. As we were doing the engine checks, the man in the tower called.

"Lockheed Two Three Seven. You will return to the ramp."

"Why?" asked Payne. We were already late and the ramp was halfway across the airport.

"You must pay the landing fee."

"Tell him I signed a paper for that and PAA will pay them."

Payne relayed that message but an even more excited voice came over the earphones.

"Lockheed Two Three Seven, return to the ramp."

At the ramp we left the right engine running. I got out and wrote a note on the landing-fee paper indicating PAA was to be billed. Also I included my home address. Reluctantly, they agreed to let us take off.

Once airborne and flying eastward over the island chain that is Indonesia, it was easy to forget the red tape of Djkharta. After we left Java, clouds formed over the islands until only the mountains poked their ten- and twelve-thousand foot peaks through. We flew above the overcast and offshore, while Polhemus continually plotted our position. His good cheer was infectious. It was amazing how we four with such varied interests worked together smoothly. However, the common interest was aviation and the task at hand, completing a thirty-year-old flight plan with our thirty-year-old airplane.

As we passed Bali, Polhemus sang "Bali Hai" repeatedly in a not unpleasant baritone and hummed the melody as he worked. Occasionally, he treated Payne and me to a chorus over the interphone.

I sent the following note to Polhemus.

> From: Captain Pellegreno
> To: Navigator Polhemus
> Subject: Wreath
> Duties: Polhemus to find suitable greenery at Lae and make wreath to drop over Howland Island. Wreath to be completed no later than 1840/01 and above assignment shall not interfere with already assigned duties.

The reply:

> From: Navigator Polhemus
> To: Captain Pellegreno
> Subject: Wreath, making of
>   1. Message rec'd, noted, and filed.
>   2. AFReq 104-76, dtd July 1903 requires that development on non-U.S. funded materials be authorized by AFIC and noted on form 617-239.

3. Funds appropriated under AFR 622 must be reallocated by suitable documentation.
4. PAI stands ready to serve, otherwise.

I knew we would have a wreath!

Since we had started on this 1190-mile flight to Kupang, located on the southern coast of Timor, Polhemus had been worried we might not make it before dark. He had calculated the usual point of no return and not until we had passed this mark and the groundspeed had not further decreased did he relax even slightly. At 6:15 we sighted the coral runway. A horse was grazing on the grass which poked through the coral, so we buzzed him. He galloped away and then we circled and landed.

At the airport office, an old wooden building, I asked the man in charge about getting gasoline.

"Oh. The gasoline man has gone home. We did not know when you were coming. Our radio had not been working properly. I think you will stay until tomorrow morning."

"We are scheduled to land at Darwin tonight," I told him. "Our clearance from Djkharta said this was a fuel stop."

"No. I'm sorry. You will have to wait until morning." He smiled, but the smile seemed remote. I did not feel like smiling in return.

Outside, I told Payne the problem. By now a half dozen men had gathered. Fifteen minutes later Payne had convinced them that we wanted gasoline now, and that the clearance was valid and correct. In an hour we wanted to be en route to Darwin! I think the military-looking flight suit he wore might have helped some, but most importantly, Payne could be exceedingly correct, polite, and stubborn—all at the same time. He was all three until he had been told the gasoline man would be fetched and that we could then depart. By that time it was dark.

Lee grabbed the chamois bucket strainer for the fuel, and in walking from the pump toward the plane stumbled in a small ditch. The audience, now expanded to include a group of children, laughed. But, this was only the beginning of the show we put on for them!

Six boys started swinging the handle of the pump for the underground storage tank. Though I would have liked to take a picture, we had been "requested" to leave our cameras aboard.

Polhemus and I went inside and started the formalities with the man who had wanted us to remain until the next morning and his assistant. They spoke English fairly well, and communication in that respect was no problem.

When I went outside to obtain Lee's and Payne's passports, they had filled the right wing tanks and had begun on the left ones, no longer using the chamois because no impurities had been found in the fuel they had put in the right wing.

I climbed up on the left wing. Some gasoline was spilled as the main tank overflowed and the footing became precarious— like water on ice! None of us moved, knowing that it would start us sliding toward the trailing edge of the wing. They handed me their passports and we waited for the fuel to evaporate. Lee and Payne finished fueling carefully. Then Lee decided to get down. As soon as he started down the backside of the wing, he began slipping, faster and faster. Then he shot off the trailing edge, barely landing on his feet. The audience was delighted. I was next. I too skidded rapidly down the wing, but Lee's steady hand braked my slide and I stepped, not too gracefully, from the wing. The people laughed. Payne followed for an encore. The show was over!

In the airport office the receipt for the gasoline was made out for 123 kilograms. That couldn't be! Taking a flashlight I walked to the pump. The reading showed 423 kilograms. Eighty-nine gallons!

The assistant wrote another receipt in his neat script and included the landing fee of $12.50 in Indonesian money.

"That comes to $82.50 you owe us," he said.

Polhemus gave him the Shell carnet. The assistant shook his head.

"What about traveler's checks?" Polhemus asked.

"We have to send them to Djkharta to get the money. We want U.S. dollars."

Polhemus put some money in the kitty. I contributed all my money and then went outside where Payne and Lee were waiting.

"What now?" they asked in unison. I told them. Each contributed and a few minutes later the receipt was signed PAID.

There were no runway lights and the rotating beacon wasn't working. Airport facilities were maintained with very few tools and perhaps beacon repair was not in the line of duty. We gave the men the rest of our Indonesian money, about $8 American, in exchange for having them drive the jeep to the inland end of the runway and shine the lights toward the seaward end where we would be.

Polhemus stepped outside the building. "Just look at those stars," he said. "And feel that soft breeze. This has been an adventure stopping here."

The darkness of the tropical night did magnify each star, and I had to admit adventure had prevailed, but the thought remained: we might have been delayed a day, in which case it would be impossible to reach Howland Island in time.

Lee made certain no one was near the propellers when the engines were started and then jumped into the plane. The jeep, loaded with all the men it could carry, started for the runway. The Lockheed moved slowly on the taxiway which intersected the runway at a right angle. It was so dark we crossed the runway without seeing it. As we turned to get back on, the plane bumped on the uneven ground, one wheel lurching into an especially deep hollow before we reached the runway.

When the electric motors were operating to pull the landing gear up, the ammeters were pegged. Therefore, only the taxi light, and not the larger and brighter landing lights, would be used, as the runway was short and the gear must come up to reduce drag as soon as the wheels lifted. Beyond the inland end of the runway rose the black silhouettes of the hills. Because of a rise in the middle of the runway we couldn't see the jeep, only the shafts the headlights sent upward.

Brakes were held and the throttles advanced to give 36.5 inches of manifold pressure. When the brakes were released, the plane moved forward, gaining momentum, the taxi light puncturing the black night. The coral became a blur and the plane rose— zooming over the jeep, barely 10 feet in the air, its gear coming up. Turning left almost immediately, we headed seaward to avoid the hills, their tops a lighter gray, the valleys night itself.

"Now that we're on our way," said Polhemus, "you wouldn't have missed it. Right?" We agreed.

The route to Darwin lay over open water, approximately 500 miles of it, a distance that would have left the engines running on fumes had we not stopped at Kupang.

Before glimpsing the Australian coast, we saw the glow from Darwin and the airport beacon flashing green and white. Something enhances the welcoming atmosphere of an airport at night—is it the lights marking the runways and taxiways, or is it knowing that wheels can safely touch the ground?

When we pulled up in front of the administration building, Lee and Polhemus jumped quickly from the plane. While Payne and I were completing the shut-down checklist, a mist floated toward the cockpit from the fuselage, engulfing us—a terrible smelling insect spray! We coughed, choked, breathed as little as possible, and charged over the tanks and out the door. Lee and Polhemus were smiling. Payne and I glared. The health officer welcomed us. Some welcome, I thought, almost preferring the one of the previous evening.

At the medical station on the airport, we were examined, even our mouths were checked. Being hungry, I thought the wooden tongue depresser looked edible. We had had no lunch or dinner and it was nearly midnight.

In exchange for $4 we were issued a medical-clearance certificate valid until we left Australian territory at which time it would be surrendered.

Immigration and customs were routine. Two reporters were waiting to talk with us. I bargained: "We'll talk on the way in to the hotel." They drove us to the hotel.

Paul Weston, the eighteen-year-old clerk at the hotel, made sandwiches from local cheese and brought trays to our rooms. He apologized for having only local cheese, but I wouldn't have traded it for all the fancy cuisine in the world.

PORT MORESBY
LAE

AUSTRALIA WAS LIKE HOME in some respects. The milk was cold and delicious and we could understand everything being said even though the accent was delightfully different.

Sunlight was glinting off the wings of the Lockheed when we arrived at half-past nine and several men were waiting for us: Group Captain, G. G. "Digger" Shiells, Officer Commanding, RAAF Base-Darwin; Frank Collopy, Regional Director of the Department of Civil Aviation (DCA); Mr. Burgoyne, the airport manager. They were given a thorough tour of the plane, and after emerging from the cramped interior, Frank Collopy said, "Just name it. It's in that airplane."

Collopy told me his brother Jim had been District Superintendent of Civil Aviation in New Guinea and had been at Lae when Earhart was. I wrote some questions and Frank said his brother would be happy to answer them if he could.

Payne and Polhemus had been given a folder containing a weather map and cloud-and-winds-aloft predictions for the 1339-mile flight to Lae. When the clearance came, we hated to leave, but the sky beckoned. Although the plane was over gross, the take-off roll was shorter than usual because a 10-knot wind was blowing down the runway. Turning east, we flew across gently undulating hills with level areas between. This was the dry season and only in some low spots was the grass green. This Northern Territory along the coast was desolate with seldom even a dirt road.

We crossed the Gulf of Carpenteria and then the

northernmost tip of the down-under continent, the Cape York Peninsula. Just north of this was Booby Island, a tiny piece of earth holding the Booby Island radio beacon on which we were homing with the ADF.

"How about sending the captain down there to live?" Polhemus called over the interphone.

"We could drop her into the water there," Payne added.

Lee just grinned. Was a mutiny forthcoming? Fortunately, Booby Island disappeared under a cloud as we flew over.

"Sorry, fellows," I said. "You know that regulations prohibit parachute jumps through clouds."

"Who said anything about a parachute?" Polhemus hollered.

East of Booby Island was the Coral Sea. Ahead was a cloud deck stretching into the distance, a white coverlet over blue water.

A while later Polhemus informed us that the flight plan had been changed to Port Moresby. No night landings were allowed at Lae. That would put us a day behind. Polhemus radioed, asking why we had not been informed when we had filed. If we had known this we would have left at dawn. If only someone had mentioned this! If only we had considered this possibility and inquired! The authorities were adamant: no night landing at Lae.

Halfway across the Coral Sea, we were told that thunderstorms had been reported in the vicinity of the pass to Lae through the Owen Stanley Range. Then clouds below us developed into a solid layer of stratus which meant an instrument approach at Port Moresby. When darkness came, we forced it back a little by turning on the instrument lights. In the distance and to our left lightning forked across the sky—the forecast storms!

Approaching our destination, we were cleared from 7000 feet and soon gray mists engulfed the plane. Over the radio beacon we turned seaward, losing altitude continually. Breaking out beneath the cloud layer, we saw the long, well-lighted runway at Jackson's Airport. The flight had taken 7 hours and 20 minutes.

In spite of the light rain, newsmen and others were waiting

in front of the new tower building. We talked with them briefly, holding jackets overhead, and since we had needed briefing for tomorrow's flight and to finalize plans for the flight to Howland, they took us to the weather bureau.

The problem was the routing to Howland. We had sufficient fuel capacity to fly nonstop from Lae to Howland, but there was no longer a suitable landing place on the island. Our destination after Howland would be Canton Island, 421 miles to the southeast. An intermediate landing point had to be chosen. Tawara, in the Gilberts, had been considered, but we had difficulty locating the proper person to contact for permission to land and take on fuel. We chose Nauru Island where arrival and departure procedures were simple, fuel was available in drums, and a radio beacon would be activated on prior request.

Weather bureau personnel contacted Nauru requesting permission to land. The notices about the Nauru landing strip included, "Be cautious to avoid masts of ships anchored just off the approach end of the runway."

We had spent more than an hour with the weather bureau personnel. It was late, so the newsmen agreed to finish their interviews in the morning and drove us to the Gateway Motel. The rooms were air conditioned and tastefully furnished. We changed clothes and then met Bill Heape, the Shell man, and some of the newsmen in the lounge. How quickly the people at each stop became friends. This was one of the very satisfying things about the flight—meeting strangers and leaving friends.

The next morning the reporters arrived the same time as my bacon and eggs, but the men insisted I finish eating first. After asking the carpenters who were finishing work on the motel to stop hammering for a few minutes, we sat on the wide front porch and taped interviews.

Polhemus left with Bill Heape to buy a larger flashlight for the nav station and find a wreath. The newsmen drove Payne, Lee, and me to the airport. As soon as we had been briefed on weather and filed a flight plan to Lae we sat under the wing to wait for Polhemus. Two more interviews were taped: one with Peter Frye, Supervisor of Talks with the Australian Broadcasting System, and one with Francis Damien, a New Guinean who was the talks correspondent for the ABC at Port Moresby. The people wanted to see one of our flight covers. Due to the humidity and heat, my slacks stuck to my legs and when I jumped into the plane there was a resounding ripping sound. The damage to my only pair of slacks was a seven-inch rip front and center.

There was no sewing kit aboard, so, casually holding my shorts in front, I walked slowly toward the terminal. The fourth person asked produced some bright red thread and a needle, and in a small room I sewed the tear. When I put on the slacks again, the red stitches showed, but I didn't mind. I knew the fond memory I would have every time I saw them after returning home.

Polhemus returned with the flashlight and wreath. The leaves were brilliant reds, yellows, and greens and in the center was a white card on which we wrote: In memory of Amelia Earhart and Fred Noonan—1937.

Then Polhemus gave Lee a funnel and a lead sinker. "Don't look so puzzled," he said. "The airlines use them instead of the drag cones. Last longer and cost less."

Lee removed the drag cone, slipped the funnel on the wire and attached the sinker to hold the funnel in place.

The storms of the previous night had dissipated, leaving only sunshine. We departed on a heading of 51 degrees for the pass between mountains towering 12 and 13 thousand feet. Indeed, the large island looks like a sleeping dragon with the jagged peaks as a backbone. Mountains and swampy lowlands dominate the terrain. Much of the island has never been explored and some sections are marked on the charts as, "relief data incomplete."

On our approach to the pass, the ground rose beneath us. Knowing the rapidity with which clouds can build and block this gateway, we were relieved to see only scattered clouds.

The jungle, dense and dark green, crept up the slopes, but above the timberline, barren peaks stretched skyward. There were almost no breaks in the green carpet below—no clearings, no trails. Once, however, we saw the dappled reflection of light on water, a river whose banks were not visible. On the other

LAE, NEW GUINEA: Approaching air field, June 30, 1967.

side of the pass, we turned toward Lae, flying along a coast where no plain welcomed the traveler and the mountains ran to the water's edge. At 7000 feet we flew toward a place which had been only a distant spot on our charts a month ago. As we finished talking with Andrews and receiving primary and secondary frequencies for the following day, we saw Lae, just east of the Markham River which empties into the Huon Gulf. Descending, we were informed that many people had gathered to welcome us. This was the last place Amelia Earhart had been officially seen.

After we flew over the airport at 500 feet, Payne, with no urging, did one of his "runway-scraping" fly-bys. I kept the movie camera rolling and fought the urge to tuck up my feet, for any moment the propellers might tick the asphalt surface of the runway.

Then I climbed the Lockheed several hundred feet, swung on final, and saw the runway ahead stretching toward the Huon

LAE, NEW GUINEA: After landing, June 30, 1967. (Courtesy Papua-New Guinea Post-Courier)

Gulf. The air was choppy over the inland end of the runway, and as I flew over the threshold, I told myself, "Easy now. Watch that airspeed. Don't let the tail get too low." The wheels touched. The plane bounced back into the air. They touched again. The third time they stuck firmly. In front of all those people, I had bounced—a miserable landing and never would my crew let me use the excitement of arriving at Lae for an excuse. Also, Lee would inspect the landing gear carefully.

After jumping from the plane, we shook hands with Jack Raynor from Shell and Mr. Bartsch, the commercial manager of Ansett Airline. About four hundred people crowded around the Lockheed. I talked with many of them including 30 girls who had walked three miles from Lae Technical College. Their names filled a page in my notebook. When I joked with their headmaster about his having ridden in a car while the girls had walked, the students giggled.

It was suggested that the Lockheed be taxied to the Guinea Airways hangar, nearer the seaward end of the runway. Soon the nose of the plane was inside the hangar though the tail was still in the sunshine. The town's picture files produced a photograph of Earhart's plane, parked no more than 5 feet from where ours was, also nose inside the hangar.

LAE, NEW GUINEA: Showing the Earhart wreath to the thirty girls from Lae Technical College. (Courtesy Papua-New Guinea Post-Courier)

Mr. Johnstone, the postmaster, took the Lae covers, saying they would be stamped and cancelled by evening with a special Earhart commemorative cancellation.

A man brought the "Official War History of Australia" and showed us pictures of Lae before and after the bombing of World War II which had destroyed everything but one house and the hangar where our plane was. The hangar had been rebuilt around the trusses, but even now steel members which had been bent by shell hits were visible.

George Griffiths introduced his wife "Tony," who had some pictures which showed Earhart, Noonan, and some people from Lae. Although we had just met, "Tony" offered to let me take the pictures back to the States, have them copied, and then return them by mail. She had witnessed Earhart's departure, seeing the plane move slowly on the take-off roll and then when it was past the end of the runway, disappear below the drop off. For some time it had remained out of sight before coming into view, climbing on course.

A half dozen New Guineans began washing our plane, swabbing the fuselage with rags and then hosing it with water. Payne and I went to the weather bureau and spent half an hour talking with the man on duty who said we could not leave before official daybreak, 6:00 a.m. We had hoped to depart earlier to insure our ETA at Howland.

The owners of the Huon Gulf Motel fixed us some sandwiches for lunch and offered to have our laundry done in town. Payne and Polhemus then left to purchase some things. Lee returned to the hangar and I waited for Bertie Heath, a pilot who had witnessed Earhart's take off. After our arrival he had introduced himself, but talk then was out of the question. Promptly at 3:00 he entered the lounge and ordered a beer. Now seventy-two years young, Bertie had started flying in 1917 and had flown DH-9's in bombing raids in France and Palestine during the First World War. He had the lean figure of a man who didn't spend much time sitting. "I still play eighteen holes of golf and don't even puff," he told me.

After taking a sip of beer, he continued, "I came to Lae in 1931. Flew supplies to the gold mines at Bulolo. Took about half an hour each way in a tri-motored Junkers."

"Do you still fly?" I asked.

"No. I quit after forty-nine years of it. But I had some real experiences. The first time I saw Japanese planes they forced me down. About February or so in 1942 I was flying a Junkers with 6000 pounds of beer for the mine crews and three Zeroes came at me. I crashed and every bottle was broken. All that beer went to waste!"

"You mentioned meeting Earhart and Noonan."

"They landed about half-past four in the afternoon. That evening Noonan and a bunch of us had some drinks and sat talking airplanes. People too."

"I'll bet you told your share of stories."

"Well, I told a few," Bertie admitted, laughing. "It was well after midnight and all of us were feeling pretty good when

LAE, NEW GUINEA: Talking with Bertie Heath, pilot who witnessed Earhart's take off from Lae in 1937.

we took Fred to the hotel. He thought they would be leaving the next day."

"They didn't though."

"No. They stayed two nights. I wondered why they didn't leave that first morning. Weather probably. And they had that ocean to cross."

He sat quietly a moment. "I wanted to see them off, but couldn't just stop working. The rest of that day I flew back and forth to the mines. The following day when returning from my first trip, I saw her silver plane move slowly down the unpaved runway. It must have been 3000 feet long at that time. When her plane reached the road that had a high crest and ran across the runway near the seaward end, it bounced into the air, went over the drop off and then flew so low over the water that the propellers were throwing spray." He paused and took a sip of beer. "Always have a couple glasses of beer every day."

"She continued straight out to sea for several miles before climbing on course slowly. That was the last I saw of her."

He thought a moment. "The wind was calm and the dust from where she had hit the crown of that dirt road didn't disperse quickly, just sort of hung there. There were other people who saw her leave. One was Lou Joubert, manager of Bulolo Gold Dredging." Bertie stared at his glass, gently swirling the amber liquid. "That was too bad, them disappearing like that."

"Yes," I agreed. "They should have made it all right. Your being a pilot—well, you would have observed carefully the things about her take off. I do appreciate your coming by to visit."

"No trouble. Enjoyed it. Time to go home for a bit of a nap. Then I'll go to the Club for their beer and chips. Best in the Territory!"

NAURU ISLAND

LAE, NEW GUINEA. JULY 1, 1967. Official daybreak was 6:00 a.m. and though we had asked, the officials would not allow us to depart one second earlier, for in this part of the world even the airlines do not fly at night. The flight plan had been filed to Canton Island, via Howland with a fuel stop at Nauru Island. The total distance was 3018 miles.

As we waited, engines ticking quietly, I looked down the 5800 feet of Runway 14 stretching toward the Huon Gulf. Take off in the opposite direction was impossible because terrain sloped up to 3200 feet within three miles. Almost every foot of runway would be needed, maybe even part of the 50-foot overrun. The slight downgrade of .7 might compensate slightly for the light offshore wind which would be with us on take off.

The sky lightened and the blue taxiway lights seemed less bright. Lee crouched behind the cockpit, hand on the dump valve. The first fifteen minutes aloft were so critical.

The seconds ticked away. A minute to go. Payne and I were strapped in with seat belts and shoulder harnesses. Ten seconds, nine, eight. The tower man would clear us at exactly 6:00. Four seconds.

Brakes held. Throttles forward to 36.5 inches of manifold. Engines throbbing, the plane quivered.

We tensed as the brakes were released. At first, movement was barely perceptible and then the plane, engines snarling, trundled slowly toward the Huon Gulf. When three quarters of the runway had been used, the tail rose. Two hundred feet from the end of the runway, Lockheed struggled into the air. Before the wheels were fully retracted the plane thundered over the water. An engine failure now meant ditching in the Huon Gulf. Gradually the distance between the silver wings and the whitecaps widened. Power was reduced to 30 inches, the propellers synchronized at 2100 rpms, and indicated airspeed hovered around 100. Even with full nose-down trim, constant forward pressure had to be held on the yoke. If the controls had been released, the plane would have stalled as the nose rose and the airspeed fell. Twenty minutes after take off, we breathed almost normally again. The altimeter registered 1000 feet! With normal gross weight the plane would have reached that altitude in less than two minutes. 2001 Zulu was listed on Polhemus's log for the time off.

With mountains on our left, we flew eastward. The sky ahead glowed with the promise of sunrise, but already clouds had gathered on that horizon. Half an hour after leaving Lae, we were over Tami Islands, just off the coast from Finsch-hafen. The Lockheed still responded heavily to the air currents, moving through them with almost no flex of the wings. Although engines were running at above normal cruise power, indicated airspeed was only 120 mph.

Golden shafts of sunlight streaked upward from the clouds massed to the east. The weather briefing at Lae had shown headwinds at 7000 feet from 140 degrees at 10 knots. As we neared Nauru they would swing more on our nose, 110 degrees, and increase to 15 knots. Forecast for the first 500 miles were periods of rain with visibility reduced to a half mile in the storms. Cumulus, towering to 30,000 feet, and stratus clouds would provide little opportunity for celestial navigation during the initial portion of the flight, but the last 1000 miles to Nauru would have less cloud cover.

The two meteorologists at Lae, J. Burns, and Bob Jones, had been exceedingly patient and helpful. Shortly before take off they had given me an envelope containing a silver spoon and the message, "Good luck and best wishes for a successful flight." Mr. Johnstone, the postmaster, had stamped and cancelled the Lae covers which were in the wing lockers.

NAURU ISLAND

The weather forecast proved correct. Two and a half hours after take off and before we had crossed the arm of the Solomon Sea which separates New Guinea from New Britain, the nose of the Lockheed skimmed through rain clouds. The clouds darkened, and visibility was less than predicted. Rivulets streamed down the windshield. Polhemus, depending on dead reckoning, plotted a position every ten minutes and labeled it the most probable. The course to Nauru lay across the southern edge of New Britain which boasted the rugged mountains of the Whiteman Range rising above 6000 feet. Our altitude was 3000 feet, and the wind, from 140 degrees, would drift us toward the island. Polhemus changed our heading slightly to the right so the Lockheed would pass south of the island.

We had left Lae at 2001 Zulu. At 2330 Zulu the clouds parted enough to allow Polhemus an astro shot, and then closed above us again. As a result of Polhemus's earlier correction to miss New Britain, we crossed the northern tip of Buka Island, 26 miles south of course.

The frequency of the radio beacon at Nauru which we had requested turned on was 335 kilocycles. As we tried to tune this, another more powerful signal came in. In the background we heard in code a faint "NI", which were the identifiers for the Nauru beacon. Looking through the radio-facility book we found that the stronger signal was from the radio beacon on Canton Island—beyond Howland Island. We tuned the ADF carefully to the Nauru beacon. Although we could hear the audio signal, it wasn't strong enough yet to home on.

An hour later the rains stopped, the clouds parted, and the South Pacific sunshine broke through. Ahead were breakers cascading against a miniature barrier reef—an almost perfect double circle with several small islands on the perimeter. From Carteret Islands, as they are called, was only ocean on our direct course to Nauru.

Several times we changed headings to circumnavigate localized storms. Generally Polhemus was able to navigate by shooting the sun which shone through thin streaks of alto cumulus. He was pleased that the remote indicating compass

EN ROUTE to Nauru: Flying through the rain. Payne and I always wore earplugs when airborne.

at the nav station was accurate to within a degree and a half. As the line on his chart stretched nearer Nauru, the radio signal became stronger. So exact was Polhemus's navigation that when the ADF needle pointed to Nauru, our heading wasn't changed one degree!

The highest point on Nauru, only 12 miles in circumference, is 220 feet, so spotting it was more difficult than the 12,000-foot peaks of the Canary Islands, but finally we saw what our ADF needle had been pointing to—a faint gray smudge on the horizon. Starting our descent, we notified Andrews that we would be out of contact for three hours. The gray smudge gradually became a green island ringed with sandy beach. Ten hours and forty-one minutes and 1452 miles after leaving Lae, the wheels touched the unpaved airstrip on the southwest coast. We taxied toward a group of Nauruans and Australians who were waiting alongside the runway.

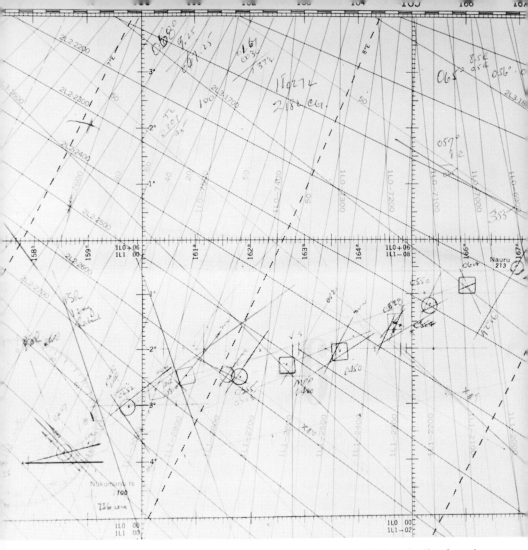

CHART SEGMENT showing latter half of navigation from Lae, New Guinea, to Nauru Island. July 1, 1967.

"Welcome to Nauru," said Mr. Vizard, the Australian administrator. "Your arrival is quite an event as we have a mail boat once a month."

Perhaps four hundred people ringed the Lockheed, looking at us and the plane with a great deal of friendly curiosity. Passports and immunization records were checked. Fred Reeve, the wireless operator, handed me a wiregram containing weather for Howland and Canton.

150

AHEAD was the airstrip at Nauru, 5300 feet long and unpaved.

Two school girls came forward carrying floral circlets of frangipani, a fragrant tropical flower. Madeline Dube, a Nauruan, placed one on Lee's head and one on mine. Leigh Miller, daughter of one of the Australian officials, crowned Payne and Polhemus. This was certainly a South Seas welcome!

Payne left to inquire about flight operations and to convince the officials that we must leave after dark to reach Howland at the desired time, and Lee requested fuel for the plane. Polhemus and I accompanied the Australians to a building where an interview was taped for the Australian Broadcasting System by the Reverend Mr. Matthews, pastor of the Nauru Protestant Church.

When we returned to the plane, a floodlight illuminated the fuel truck loaded with barrels and parked near the fuselage door. Swinging a pump handle back and forth rapidly was a young Nauruan who had tapped one of the barrels. Since there was no nozzle on the hose, Lee would shout, "Stop!" to shut off the flow each time a tank was full. Once he didn't yell soon enough and gasoline overflowed in the fuselage. Quickly he opened the floorboards so the fuel could evaporate. Lee never liked fueling the fuselage tanks, standing inside among those

AT NAURU, people ringed the plane and looked at us with friendly curiosity.

fumes, aware that a small spark, metal against metal, could produce an inferno.

Our tank installation was exceptionally clean and odor free. The recommended procedure was to put a rag around the filler neck so any spilled fuel would be absorbed. This time, the fuel had come too quickly and the entire fuselage smelled like a gasoline tank.

When the fueling was completed, Leigh's parents, Ken and Judy Miller, drove us to the compound where unmarried personnel reside. Once the car lurched to the left and I saw a pig scurry into the brush.

"That was one of a herd of forty or so that roams the island," Judy told us.

At the compound, Jessie Barraclough, the hostess, led us to dinner. Generous helpings of chicken, mashed potatoes, peas, and pie disappeared quickly while we read the report of our flight in the Pinnacle Post, the daily Nauruan newspaper.

The soft tropical breeze and the friendly people we would like to know better tempted us to linger, but we returned to the airstrip. Payne had persuaded the authorities to allow the second night take off in the history of the island. Arrangements were made to pay for the fuel and fueling costs, but we were later notified that the Australian Government of Nauru had paid these charges for us. Such a welcome contribution this was!

The airstrip had been transformed into a narrow corridor outlined by flarepots on both sides. Many of the people who had watched us arrive now returned to see the silver plane disappear into the night.

When we taxied toward the end of the runway, a jeep preceded us to check for pigs. Then the driver returned to the opposite end of the runway from where he would flash his headlights three times to indicate the runway was clear for departure.

As we turned into position for take off, clouds of dust swirled behind from the propeller blast. Ahead of us stretched the 5300-foot unpaved runway. The jeep's lights blinked three times. Again, only the taxi light was used, for the gear had to come up immediately after lift off. The engines roared their challenge to the tropical night and as the last flarepot was passed, the Lockheed rose. Then we were over the Pacific, clinging to our precious few feet of altitude and proceeding on instruments because over water at night there is no visible horizon.

This night was almost magical, with stars our guiding lights for a rendezvous with history. The silver plane climbed slowly on course. Destination—Howland Island.

HOWLAND ISLAND

SILVER WINGS SLICED through the heavy dark velvet of the tropical night toward a pinpoint of land 1145 miles distant. How close the stars seemed, yet how remote they were.

One clear October night a long time ago I had gazed upward. For a moment I was aware only of vast incomprehensible distance. Although I could locate the familiar constellations, the knowledge of their infinite distances from earth made me feel more alone than ever before. Overwhelmed by the immensity of the universe, I shivered at the thought that earth was a mere speck and I an infinitesimally minute fraction of that speck. The shiver, however, was replaced with a wonderful feeling of warmth when I realized that to be alive and a comprehending part of the earth system was almost a miracle in itself.

And now, an airplane carried four humans guided by the stars. Our platform was a product of more than thirty years of progress since the first powered flight. By now we knew the Lockheed well: the fuel transfer, the power settings and cruise altitudes. We knew the sound of converters whirring when we transmitted on the HF, the high whine of the inverter when we needed 110-volt AC, the two-minute intervals when we held the plane level for astro shots. And always the throb of the engines was there, conveying the feeling that the plane was alive beneath our feet. I looked out the window through the shining propeller arc to the dark ocean below.

The vast Pacific—the endless Pacific as it must have seemed to the ancient mariners—is an ocean larger than the combined land masses of the earth, constituting over half the water surface of the earth. The number of islands runs to the tens of thousands—more islands than all other oceans and seas combined, and so many as to have never been counted. Of all these islands, very few are named.

In spite of the vast number of islands, the pilot flying over this ocean hour after hour sees only limitless water. Even the "island constellations" do not shatter this illusion, for often only one island in them is visible at a time, so distant are these pinpoints, so often cloud shrouded.

One of the pinpoints is Howland Island. Its nearest neighbor, Baker Island, is approximately 50 miles south and slightly larger. However, one could not call the two islands a constellation in any sense. Their nearest neighbors (except for a sand bar about 100 miles southeast) are the Phoenix Islands, slightly over 400 miles southeast. Six hundred miles to the west are the Gilbert Islands and 800 miles to the northwest lie the Marshall Islands.

We were putting our faith in the chart makers. Before World War II, accurate maps of the Pacific were unavailable. Later mapping put more pinpoints nearer their correct positions. But even on the charts we used, none dated earlier than 1966, there were notations: Stewart Island (reported about 13 miles east), Nijuna (reported 3 miles northeast in 1926), Maraki (true position of island may vary 10 miles). This vast ocean is broken only by the bits of coral, atolls, and islands, and even these are not charted accurately.

Polhemus took astro shots periodically, sometimes at fifteen-minute intervals, sometimes at half-hour or forty-five minute ones. Each time he would precompute three stars. When the time came for him to shoot, the plane's heading and altitude had to be held constant and the wings level for two minutes. Always having to add a little right aileron made this a bit of a problem, but we allowed the difficulty to interfere as little as possible. At the end of these two-minute intervals required for the averaging mechanism in the sextant, I always breathed deeply, having practically held my breath during them.

At 1200 Zulu our estimated position was 23 miles west of the 170th meridian of east longitude and about 17 miles south of the equator. At 1340 Zulu Polhemus said we were about 100 miles south of Tarawa in the Gilberts and slightly more than 700 miles from Howland.

Our reason for leaving Lae on July 1 instead of July 2 as Earhart had done was to be airborne and nearing Howland at the time the Ninety-Nines—an international organization of women pilots—as part of their international convention, would be holding services at the Smithsonian Institution in commemoration of the thirtieth anniversary of Amelia Earhart's last flight. Women from Australia, Canada, the Netherlands, South Africa, India, Pakistan, Brazil, Greece, England, Morocco, and the Philippines were expected to attend.

After deciding what to include in the message which would be broadcast to the group, I relaxed in Lee's seat. Since there was less engine noise at the nav station, we transmitted from there when sending anything but routine messages.

Always I was amazed at the tiredness that invited instant sleep as soon as I wasn't actively engaged. The next thing I knew Polhemus was punching me on the arm. "Time to wake up. It'll be 1600 Zulu in five minutes. That's noon in Washington."

I dozed again, in spite of the excitement and anticipation of sending this message.

"Hey. Wake up!" Polhemus shook me again. "Andrews is reading us loud and clear and they're working on the phone patch into the Smithsonian."

It was a strange feeling knowing that my voice would be heard 7000 miles away. I was affected even more strangely by the knowledge that we were sending from a platform about 400 miles west of Howland and 7000 feet above the Pacific. And to think the auditorium at the Smithsonian would be filled mostly with people whom I had never met—but they were pilots and that united us. At the moment I felt an even stronger bond in realizing that they were paying tribute to Amelia Earhart on the thirtieth anniversary of her last flight, and I, in another way, was doing the same. Polhemus handed me the microphone.

"Ninety-Nines and Mrs. Morrissey. Thirty years ago another silver Lockheed 10 was flying toward Howland Island about this time. In essence we've been back in that year, 1937. We've thought about Amelia Earhart and other aviation pioneers. Along with these thoughts has come the realization of the tremendous undertaking an around-the-world flight was in 1937. My navigator has worked out a sun line, the same one Amelia was working and we will attempt to find Howland using the method used during the 1937 flight. Presently, we are about 400 miles west of Howland and hope you will join us in spirit during the time we are over Howland which will be approximately 1900 Zulu, or 3:00 p.m. your time."

Then we signed off with Andrews. Later I found that several Ninety-Nines had replied to the message but no one had told us to listen for an answer.

We were going to use the sun-line-landfall technique Noonan had in all probability been depending upon. However, we had the advantage of a superior sextant, and by tuning WWV, Polhemus could obtain a time hack almost instantly. He also had the Sight Reduction Tables used for rapid solution of the trigonometry involved in celestial shots. The successful completion of this leg depended on Polhemus, as the 1937 flight had depended upon Fred Noonan.

So far the weather had been as predicted in the Nauru wiregram: scattered rainshowers, but not enough to hinder astro navigation. Sometimes we flew through lighter looking clouds but always flew around the larger buildups.

After sending the message to the Ninety-Nines, I returned to the cockpit to await dawn. When the eastern sky lightened, I looked down upon rows of clouds with ocean between. At 7000 feet we were high enough to see silvery tops in all directions.

Had there been islands below which we had intended to use for checkpoints, undoubtedly we would not have been able to see them. To remain at this altitude meant that our true airspeed was greater and less fuel was burned. Also, below the clouds we could not have used celestial navigation.

At 1715 Zulu we crossed the International Date Line. Again it was July 1 for us. The illusion we had somehow made up for all the lost hours in flying east did not diminish the fatigue factor. However, the challenge of finding Howland Island kept me alert. What would the island look like? Had it changed shape since 1937—during that thirty-year span, so short a time in comparison to the eons it had been an insignificant and unknown island?

The Coast Guard cutter Blackhaw should be positioned offshore Howland Island and we started calling on its assigned HF frequency.

"Blackhaw. Blackhaw. This is Lockheed Seven Nine Two Three Seven. Do you read?" We broadcast this repeatedly. No response. Only the slight hissing of radio waves without voice was heard. How similar to the 1937 flight!

"KHAQQ CALLING ITASCA. KHAQQ CALLING ITASCA. WE ARE LISTENING ON. . . ."

"Blackhaw. Blackhaw. This is Lockheed Seven Nine Two Three Seven. Do you read?" No answer. We had never been in direct contact with this ship as arrangements had been made through the Coast Guard in Washington, D.C. A message to the Ninety-Nines was to have been sent from this ship as it was moored offshore Howland.

We called the Blackhaw again. Still no reply. Was the frequency being monitored?

Polhemus began taking celestial shots more frequently. He shot the sun at 1730, 1743, and 1755 Zulu. At 1800 Zulu he estimated our position as 125 miles west of Howland.

Celestial shots were taken at 1810 and 1820 Zulu. The line on the chart inched toward the tiny island.

Finally the Blackhaw responded to our calls. The ship had departed Howland and was cruising northeast. The frequency would continue to be monitored. I was a little disappointed the

POLHEMUS using the Kollsman periscopic sextant to shoot the sun as we neared Howland Island.

ship had left before our arrival, but knew a schedule had been assigned it.

At 1823 Zulu, Polhemus called over the interphone. "We're an estimated 60 miles west of Howland. Descend to 1000 feet and turn 30 degrees left."

Throughout the night, headings had ranged from 072 to 080 degrees and now the plane swung to 044 degrees. Following the accepted practice of sun-line-landfall technique, this heading change would allow us to be reasonably assured that when we reached the line of position Howland would lie to the right on a course of 157 degrees.

At 1855 Zulu our position was about forty-five miles north northwest of Howland. "Line of position," said Polhemus. "Turn to 157 degrees. Estimating Howland at 1915."

On all sides were scattered rainsqualls, with solid cloud walls. At this altitude, we no longer saw the fluffy topsides, and the dark areas beneath appeared menacing. Between the rains lay rippled ocean with shafts of sunlight sending diamonds sparkling. But, our view was blocked in almost every direction by the squalls. Ironically, we had to be below the clouds to find the island but for celestial navigation we would have to climb above them and risk not seeing the tiny island which could be obscured by the smallest cloud.

At 1905 Zulu (0705 local) the Lockheed was heading a steady 157 degrees, running down the line of position toward the target. At 1912 a rain squall lay directly on the flight path. Was Howland underneath that dark cloud? The only way to find out was to descend to 300 feet, fly in close, and look beneath the base of the raincloud. No small island shaped like a teardrop appeared—only gray ocean dancing with raindrops.

Not wanting to fly directly beneath the cloud and rain at a low altitude, Polhemus said, "Turn to 270 degrees. We'll fly that way for a while. Maybe we're too far east."

I banked the plane, turning away from the squall. For ten minutes we flew west, four pairs of eyes straining for the sight of a sandy island. We looked beneath and between other squalls. No island.

"Blackhaw. Blackhaw. This is Lockheed Two Three Seven. Do you read?"

"Blackhaw to Lockheed Two Three Seven. Go ahead."

"Lockheed Two Three Seven requests you key your mike so we can take a DF fix on you."

"Roger. Keying mike."

The needle of the ADF pointed to the Blackhaw, off our tail and to the right.

"Blackhaw to Two Three Seven. We're presently steaming 042 degrees and our estimated position is 37 nautical miles from Howland on a bearing of 042 degrees."

"Roger. Thank you Blackhaw."

The time was 1943 Zulu, twenty minutes past our ETA for Howland. Polhemus calculated the relative bearing to the Blackhaw. All of us looked for the island.

"Let's fly east again," Polhemus said. "We can't be that far off. According to my figures on that DF position we're west of the island and slightly north."

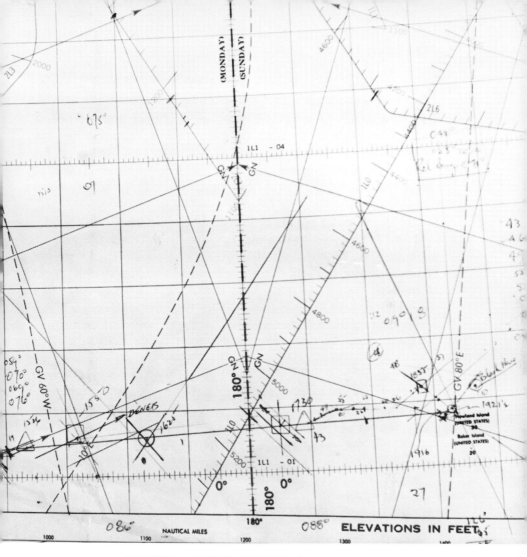

SECTION of PACIFIC OCEANIA GLC-7N showing Polhemus's navigation to Howland Island.

Heading east, we peered through the windows. Where was that island? Sunlight reflected on the open areas and danced off wave tops, sending shimmering spangles into our eyes. Was this ocean mocking us? To our right or south lay almost a continuous cloud, another squall. The sunlight seemed only an illusion between the rains. We had to find Howland Island. But, even with our superior navigation equipment, we too, were having difficulty locating the strategic island.

"We have about twenty minutes more to search and then we'll have to go on," Polhemus warned.

How defeated we would feel if we could not find the island, but how ironic that for some reason the small island defied our navigation and remained hidden. It was easy to imagine the tension Earhart and Noonan must have felt as they searched for a "safe harbor." They, too, knew their fuel could not last much longer.

Flying east, I felt on edge with tiredness and frustration—anxious to find that island, disappointed if we could not.

Lee was looking out the fuselage windows to the south, Polhemus to the north. Payne and I covered the front quadrants. All eyes strained. At times the rain splashing beneath the squalls looked like waves dashing against a distant shoreline. But, as we approached, the illusion vanished, leaving empty ocean.

Where was Howland?

I heard another message echo. "KHAQQ CALLING ITASCA. WE MUST BE ON YOU BUT CANNOT SEE YOU."

Thirty years later we had the same feeling. We must be near Howland, but where was it? The bearing taken on the Blackhaw indicated we were in the right area. Our celestial navigation had been accurate.

To the south lay a nearly continuous line of squally clouds hanging almost to the ocean, and gray curtains of rain slanted downward.

Lee tapped Payne on the shoulder. "I think I saw something through a break in the clouds. It looked like an island."

We scanned the southern horizon. Under the jagged cloud fringes we saw what Lee and seen—a bare scruff of land distant enough to look like a cloud shadow. How fitting it was that Lee had seen the island first, for the flight had been his idea.

Leaving the squalls behind, we flew south. The island did not disappear, but increased in size. We had been perhaps 10 to 12 miles north of the island when Lee had spotted it.

Howland Island was in the middle of a vast, nearly

HOWLAND ISLAND viewed from the left seat of Lockheed N79237, July 1, 1967.

cloudless area, with only a few rows of cumulus marring the blue dome. In fact, the weather was uncannily similar to what it had been in 1937 when Commander Thompson had scanned the horizon from the deck of the Itasca and seen menacing dark clouds some forty miles to the northwest.

No reef led toward this small bit of land, only a half mile wide and perhaps two miles long. The highest point is less than ten feet above sea level, another factor making it difficult to locate. Yet we had spotted Howland Island seemingly hiding from the prying eyes of those who would further disturb its slumber, the silent slumber of an underwater mountain produced by the upsurge of the ocean floor eons ago.

A shallow beach ringed the island and the one hundred-fathom line must have been very close to the shore. Thirty feet from the beach, the gray yellow of the shallow water changed to the dark blue of the abysmal Pacific, leaving the breakers behind to surge again and again against the deserted shoreline.

On the western side of the island a red and white tower houses the Earhart Beacon. Nearby is the foundation of a building which had once stood, a lonely sentinel upon this windswept isle. Those two markings reminded us that the island had not always been abandoned.

I would have liked to remain by the island longer, but Polhemus said, "Remember, we used part of the allotted time finding the island."

As we circled Howland, lying jewellike in a dark blue ocean, I felt a sense of history—an exciting feeling—and also one of extreme relief that we had found the island. This was where another Lockheed 10 should have landed thirty years ago. No trace of the three runways prepared for the other plane were visible, the scrub brush having obscured them. It was easy to imagine that high above us the ghostly silver wings of another Lockheed 10 were casting a shadow on the island which had been there in 1937 too, but was not the destiny of that other crew.

When the second circle around the island was completed, Payne took the controls and I went back to where Lee had strapped himself in his seat. I held the wreath and Lee's arms encircled me in a bearlike grip, for opening the door would create a suction toward the outside. The reds, greens, and yellows of the leaves were as bright as they had been in Port Moresby. Payne flew north of the island and then turned back, descending to 50 feet above the sea and flying slowly. Polhemus waited near the window to tell us when to drop the wreath.

"Get ready," he said. "We're over the island."

Lee rammed his foot harder against the door and wedged it open with his boot. Leaning forward, I pushed the wreath through the opening, feeling it torn from my hands. It landed on the island, hopefully where another pair of Lockheed 10 wheels should have touched thirty years ago.

CANTON ISLAND

THE WREATH HAD BEEN DROPPED at 2005 Zulu (0805 local) and by 2007 we were on course for Canton Island, 421 miles southeast. Polhemus thought that if we had kept going through that first squall encountered when nearing Howland, we probably would have been "dead on" the island. However, thinking we might have flown too far east, he had suggested flying west awhile. Then we had flown east again. Anyone on Howland this morning would have seen a small speck emerge from the clouds and gradually become a pair of silver wings.

I called Liberty Airways and requested a phone patch to the family farm in Michigan. Everyone was there! I talked with Don, my grandmother who had told newsmen that I had been a "mischievous child with big blue eyes," my parents, uncles, aunts, and cousins. They were as thrilled as I when considering the distance. Propagation was so excellent it would hardly have surprised me to see them perched on the wing just outside the cockpit window.

Half an hour southeast of Howland, I began threading through the white corridors of clouds billowing above us, bending the Lockheed around the curves, sometimes intentionally slicing through the white mists with a wing. Occasionally, I flew through small puffs, losing the sunshine momentarily but receiving a blinding stab of light when the plane emerged from the other side.

Payne napped a good deal on this leg. We were all ready to fall asleep, having been awake more than 24 hours. The half-hour nap I had taken while waiting to send the message to the Ninety-Nines had helped some, but my eyelids grew heavy and I had to force them open, trying to remain alert until we arrived at Canton.

Slightly less than three hours after we left Howland, the blue-green circular reef that was Canton lay ahead. The flight service station located on the island was contacted on 126.7 and we were given wind direction and velocity. On the basis of that information we planned a straight-in approach to the south-southeast runway which paralleled the coast.

We got out of the plane stiffly and stood up straight—what a tremendous feeling after being cramped in the plane for nearly 24 of the preceding 28 hours. Indeed, we probably appeared like slow-moving robots, so exhausted were we.

After a quick lunch in the mess hall, our host Ernie, one of a contingent on Howland who worked for a stateside corporation, took us to our quonset huts. Though the huts had metal roofs, they were cool inside and a breeze blew through the windows. On Canton the trade winds blow almost continually and keep the warmth pleasant.

I felt like sleeping the entire day we had "gained" by crossing the International Date Line. Canton Island was the ideal place for rest, relaxation, and food. As one reporter told us after the flight, "You just disappeared for two days. We didn't know where you had gone."

We slept that afternoon, but after dinner, Ernie drove us past the pits where planes had been kept during World War II and past the powerful radio beacon transmitting antenna, looking innocent enough, just wires strung between tall poles.

"That is one of the most powerful beacons in the world," Ernie told us.

"We know," I replied. "Our ADF picked up its audio signal about 2400 miles away."

Canton Island had been important in the early trans-Pacific air routes, positioned as it is between Hawaii and New Caledonia. The waters of the lagoon had been sliced many times by the hulls of the Pan American Clippers which pioneered Pacific air transportation.

That night I fell asleep listening to the heavy thumping of

the colossal diesel engines which maintained electricity for the island and were used every two weeks to make fresh water. On the other side of the hut was the soft sound of surf lapping against the beach.

The next morning Ernie took us surf fishing. He had located four poles with spinning reels. In his back yard was a palm tree. "Ten years ago," he told us, "there were no palms on the island but people planted them and now it looks like paradise. We just speeded things up instead of waiting for the currents to drift this particular vegetation to these shores. The hermit crabs which we use for bait, those pink shells in the tree, promptly adopted the palms for roosts."

We filled the bait pail, watching the hermits pull inside their "houses" when touched. Ernie followed the same road we had taken last night until it was only a trail. From where he parked the jeep, the ocean was not visible, but when we walked over the rise, the blue and gold of ocean and sand stretched to infinity. Against the bright sand, the azure of the ocean deepened, approaching violet. Voices were lost in the wind which was sweeping the whitecaps shoreward, breaking them on a sand bar about fifty feet out. A dazzling sun reflected off the water and sand. There were neither trees nor signs of civilization, only the beach meeting the ocean as it had for ages.

I burn easily, so Lee loaned me one of his long-sleeved shirts. The men wore tennis shoes, but I like waves rushing over my feet and took off my shoes and socks.

Ernie instructed me in the use of a spinning reel and the third time I tried, the line went out thirty feet but nothing was caught. The fourth cast there was a nibble. I reeled in quickly, but Ernie said that kind wasn't eaten, so my catch was thrown back.

After wading in the surf, I realized that small rocks were being thrown with some force toward the beach each time a wave curled shoreward. Soon I was wet to my hips, but was casting further and further. Payne caught a fish that was definitely edible. Then I reeled in the same kind. An hour later we had four good-sized fish, enough for a meal.

The rocks being thrown with the waves had pounded my

ankles, but being so absorbed in fishing, I had ignored the pelleting. Later when I walked toward the jeep, my ankles throbbed.

A telegram was waiting at the settlement area.

POSTMASTER CANTON ISLAND

> PLEASE REGARD THIS TELEGRAM AS AUTHOR-ITY FOR MRS. ANN PELLEGRENO NOW FLYING AMELIA EARHART ROUTE TO LODGE ONE HUN-DRED WORDS ADDRESSED PRESS COLLECT BROADNEWS PORT MORESBY STOP MANY THANKS

AUSTRALIAN BROADCASTING SYSTEM

So, even here we could not hide completely. A report of the flight since leaving New Guinea was drafted with special emphasis on Howland Island and delivered to the wireless station.

Ernie put our fish in the large refrigerator in the mess hall where everyone ate buffet style. Such delicious food too: salads, meats, fruits. At the end of the line was a big container filled with chilled juice, a different type with each meal—guava, orange, or passion fruit juice. We avoided this last one! Supplies were flown in every two weeks on a DC-8 from Honolulu.

That evening on the dock we were introduced to "Mr. Dote," a Japanese, who told us that when Earhart had been in Honolulu in 1937, he had been the captain of the boat which had ferried her back and forth between Coconut Island and Kaneohe Bay.

Skillfully, he maneuvered the boat from the dock and soon we left the lagoon behind. Three parachute lines with hooks attached were let out over the transom. This was trolling, Canton Island style. A few minutes later Payne's line jerked and he hauled in an eighteen-inch tuna. My line jerked. I was so excited I almost forgot to haul in the line. The fish was skipping out of the water.

"MR. DOTE," who had ferried Amelia Earhart in Honolulu in 1937, took us deep sea fishing and prepared a fabulous fish-fry the evening we departed.

"Haul in the fish or the sharks will get it," shouted Mr. Dote.

Hand over hand I pulled the weight of the fish plus the additional drag of the line as the boat maintained forward speed. I had never caught such a big fish—a tuna almost as long as Payne's.

The sun was almost below the horizon when black humps began moving alongside the boat. The porpoises jumped from the water, easily keeping pace with the boat, and played around for half an hour, and then as if by signal, suddenly veered away. Golden clouds spiraled upward on the western horizon and the boat moved slowly back toward the lagoon entrance.

The fish were to be shared with the people in the mess. "Just wait," said Mr. Dote. "We fix them in a special way. You'll see tomorrow evening."

The following morning my ankles were swollen and sore

from the pounding received in the surf. Feet and ankles were lobster red from even that exposure to the tropical sun. I did manage to get out of bed by noon, but my feet, almost twice their normal size, barely fit in my tennis shoes with the laces out. Payne promptly dubbed me "Red Socks."

At the flight service station one of the men gave me a cable that had been saved which told of our safe arrival in Caracas and intended departure for Paramaribo. Weather data for our evening flight to Honolulu was obtained.

Since we had to confirm the plans regarding Oakland and Newton, my crew decided to fly the plane. I wanted some movies of the Lockheed in flight, so I positioned myself alongside the runway. What a marvelous sound those two engines made as the plane roared past on take off. Then Payne flew by three times so I could shoot the movie film. As an extra, he added his "runway-scraping" fly-by!

After that, the Lockheed climbed until it was over a mile high, a small silhouette against the sky. Back and forth it flew while the phone patches were made. How odd I felt seeing that plane up there. How many other people might have seen a similar plane somewhere over the broad expanse of the Pacific in 1937.

The tuna was fixed for dinner that evening. "We call it 'sashime,' " one of the cooks told me. "We cleaned the fish and sliced them. Then we put them on this bed of cabbage. We made the sauce too. This is a real delicacy for us."

I dipped a chunk of meat in the sauce, similar to shrimp cocktail sauce. The tender uncooked tuna was delicious and completely free of the taste usually associated with canned tuna.

Our take off was scheduled for midnight. Ernie had arranged a cookout at his house because Mr. Dote wanted to cook Japanese style the fish we had caught. By eight o'clock he was building a fire. Into a shallow metal cooking dish he poured some liquids, but would not disclose exactly what they were. "Very delicious," he said. "You will see."

More liquid was added, some sugar, and finally when the mixture sputtered, he put in the fish which had been cleaned but left whole. Lee had been preflighting the plane and arrived as they were being lifted from the pan.

"Chopsticks for everyone," said Mr. Dote, and then showed us how to use them.

Those fish were absolutely delicious—from the crackling skin to the just tender flesh with a sweet-sour taste. Each of us ate half a fish and Mr. Dote beamed. He had taken good care of us, as he had done also for another pilot in 1937.

Aware that for the first time on the flight we had no schedule or pressures to arrive at Howland on time, I would have liked to enjoy longer the luxury of relaxation in this tropical paradise. But, even with more than 3000 miles of the Pacific behind us, long overwater legs to Honolulu and Oakland remained. Reluctantly, we let Ernie drive us to the quonsets to pick up our gear.

"Hurry up, Red Socks," Payne called as I went into my quonset. I gathered my luggage and was back at the jeep before he was.

Mr. Dote and Ernie waited while we readied the plane. Slightly past midnight, local time, we were in position on the runway. The tense moments of this overweight take off were somewhat eased by the presence of runway lights and a paved surface. Soon the green and white rotating beacon was behind us and we turned on course for Honolulu, 1972 miles ahead.

"Steer 032 degrees, Red Socks," said Payne.

We flew through the star-filled night, a lone silver airplane. Polhemus took celestial shots twice an hour. As the winds shifted, so did the headings—from 032, to 025, to 020 and as high as 037 degrees. When daylight came, we saw only blue water and fair-weather cumulus. Whitecaps were being whipped up, but they looked small from 7000 feet.

It was July 4th, the day Earhart had planned to be back in the States in 1937.

We felt like celebrating, because when we arrived in Honolulu we would officially be back in the States, although our longest overwater flight still separated us from the mainland.

Fourteen hours and sixteen minutes after leaving Canton, we landed at Honolulu International. Taxiing toward the Pan American gate, I knew islandic paradise and quiet lay behind me.

HONOLULU
OAKLAND
DENVER

★ ★ ★

AS SOON AS WE JUMPED FROM THE PLANE at the Pan American gate, newsmen crowded around us and asked, "Where have you been?"

We told them about Nauru, the wreath, almost not finding Howland, and Canton Island. At the hotel messages were already waiting. After flopping on the floor and stretching muscles cramped by the hours of flying I returned the calls.

Dinner was in the Surf Room at the Royal Hawaiian Hotel where my feet were tucked underneath the table. The "red socks" were still prominent and my swollen feet had been forced into the Dakar shoes with heel straps left unfastened.

On the shoreline fireworks sent red, white, and blue streamers cascading, and firebombs punctuated the dinner music. Lobster, the best I had ever eaten, disappeared quickly, for my last meal had been Mr. Dote's succulent fish.

As we four walked slowly back to our hotel, it was easy to forget the long overwater flight ahead and the hours of flying since leaving Detroit. Fireworks were still showering the beach and the air was fragrant with the smell of flowers.

More messages had been tucked under my door. After returning the calls, I switched off the air conditioner, opened the windows, and enjoyed the soft sea breeze. Having been awake more than thirty hours, I had no difficulty falling asleep in spite of the continuing Fourth of July celebrations.

The next morning Ruth Wilkins, a friend of my godmother, treated us to coconut pancakes under a huge banyan tree in the

patio of a beach hotel. What a pleasant way to eat breakfast—
the sound of the surf nearby, a gentle breeze from the ocean,
and sunlight filtering through the stately tree.

After Lee and the two Bills left for the airport, I went with
Mrs. Wilkins and her grandson to the Amelia Earhart
Memorial located on a prominence near the road which winds
up the east side of the island. The inscription on the bronze
plaque which was dedicated March 14, 1937 reads:

AMELIA EARHART
FIRST PERSON TO FLY ALONE
FROM HAWAII TO NORTH AMERICA
JANUARY 11, 1935

Back in my room, I returned more calls while waiting for
Lee Gottwald and Isabel Petronski, both members of Zonta, an
international women's service organization, who had invited
me for lunch. Amelia Earhart had been a Zontian, and the
secretary of the Ann Arbor Zonta had written the Honolulu
chapter about our flight.

Luncheon conversation centered on Amelia and her activities when she had been in Honolulu. Isabel had been present
when the famous pilot had spoken to the Honolulu Zonta. The
two women introduced me to poi, a Hawaiian dish made from
taro root which had been baked, pounded, moistened, and
fermented. As instructed, I scooped some of the gray paste
from my bowl with three fingers. The flavor was distinct, but
not one that would have stood out among spices.

The following day, July 6, I arrived at the airport at 2:00
p.m., two hours before scheduled departure time. A list of the
companies which had helped us had been painted on the
fuselage near the door. Until now we had kept the Lockheed as
Earhart's had been, an unpainted silver plane.

David Pa from the Pan American food commissary asked
what we wanted in our box lunches. I told him whatever he
thought we would like. Soon he returned with the food and a lei
of bright blue and white flowers which he placed around my
neck and then kissed me—the traditional way of bestowing
these flowered garlands in Hawaii. Such a nice way of saying
good-bye! The leis are supposed to be thrown overboard as the

ship leaves the harbor but this would have been a bit difficult for us. Not really wanting to part with the flowers, I was glad of the excuse.

This would be our longest leg, and a decision was made to ship all unnecessary items to California via commercial air freight: the spare generator, film, charts, the blanket and mattress, and pounds of general miscellany!

The news media people arrived—those from television, newspapers, magazines; men from Jeppesen and Shell; a man who had witnessed Earhart's disastrous Honolulu take off in 1937; and a student who had been in my aviation ground school back in Michigan.

Ruth Wilkins and her two daughters-in-law brought leis made from brightly colored flowers picked in their yards for each crew member.

At 0218 Zulu (4:18 p.m. Hawaiian time) the heavy Lockheed moved down the runway. Finally the wheels inched upward, and the plane, climbing slowly, turned seaward. The hotel-lined shore, Diamond Head, and the mountains hung with misty clouds were left behind and we looked ahead to ocean and sky.

There was no land between here and California, no sand bars springing out of the ocean at low tide, no minute islands. This part of the Pacific, whose waters had passed beneath the wings of Pan American Clippers and of Earhart's Vega and Lockheed 10, the wings of jets, and now beneath our silver wings had taken its toll of pilots and planes.

By our flight plan, Oakland was 2461 miles from Honolulu. Fuel aboard (800 gallons) was for an estimated 20 hours and 20 minutes. Estimated time en route was 17 hours and 20 minutes. The winds aloft were not encouraging. Headwinds from 080 degrees at 20 knots were forecast for the first part of our path. Tailwinds, slight as they would be, were not predicted until past the point of no return.

The Lockheed eased through two small rainstorms. The sun set quickly. The line on Polhemus's chart angled northeast.

After he had taken several sightings, he frowned. "The headwinds are ten knots stronger than forecast."

"You mean we might have to turn back?" I thought of the preparations made for Oakland and Newton and remembered the winds which had forced our return to Trinidad. If this increase held, the en route time would be boosted beyond our safe fuel reserve—beyond even that minimum reserve necessary when aiming at a continent!

"We'll continue as long as it's safe," Polhemus said. "The winds should break. If they would at least swing around more to the north, much of the headwind component would be cancelled."

"When's the PNR?"

"Eight point six hours from Honolulu."

Disheartened, I crawled back to the cockpit, wishing I might will the winds to break. Causing the headwinds was a huge high-pressure area lying about 600 miles northwest of our course. As our flight path was on the bottomside of the high, and since wind circulates clockwise around high pressure areas, the headwinds were ours. Hopefully, past the PNR, we would be entering the wind flow on the east side of the high which would tend to come from the north. Later, a slight tailwind component should develop. So far we had only the headwinds—and ten knots stronger than forecast. The clear sky was deceptive, and without celestial navigation capability, I could have believed the Lockheed would arrive on time at Oakland.

At 0855 Zulu we had been 6 hours and 43 minutes en route, had flown 780 miles, and our position was 150 degrees west longitude and 30 degrees north latitude. At this point we swung on a more easterly course.

After we had passed the PNR, I returned to the nav station where Polhemus was doing some rapid figuring and frowning. However, he did not tell us to turn the plane around. Almost an hour later we were still flying east. Polhemus said the headwinds had diminished slightly and the groundspeed had increased.

Always it seemed like magic when the eastern sky lightened, at first so imperceptibly that a blink of an eye might cause darkness to return. Below was an undercast, at first an inky black, and then a dark gray turning lighter gray. Along the horizon to the east were long, pencil-thin black clouds, not storm clouds, but streaks of stratus. Then the sun surged above them, sending dazzling light into the cockpit. Above us stretched angel wings of high cirrus fanning the sky between them. Later the undercast broke—a clean edge—leaving open ocean below which reached beyond the horizon to California.

Calls were received on the HF from J. P. McCarthy and the people in Newton, Kansas. We contemplated contacting those who had been skeptical about our chances of completing the flight, but didn't.

Two hundred miles out, Payne said, "Hey, Red Socks, can you see California?"

"Neg. Neg." I told him in the approved Payne fashion.

Lee came forward to "help look for the coastline."

"Any sign of land?" Polhemus called over the interphone a short while later.

"Negative," I replied.

"Are you sure you don't see the coastal ranges?" Payne asked.

"Neg. Neg."

Still I looked ahead, hoping for some sign of the coast. Tiredness was replaced by the anticipation of landing at Oakland.

A shadow finally appeared on the horizon, a long shadow which became the coast with hilltops poking above scattered clouds. Air Traffic Control requested our position so that the men from a television station who were in an airplane could take pictures. In a few minutes the "twin" flew out of the mist, stayed alongside a while, crossed in front of us, and then, waggling its wings, departed.

Radar vectored us over the Bay and on a long final for Oakland International. Down there was the same runway that Earhart had used in 1937, that we had used a month ago, and that we would land on today, July 7, 1967.

"Will you make a fly-by for the newsmen?" the man in the control tower asked.

"Roger," I told him. I flew the plane in a low pass over the runway, pulled up, and soon turned on downwind. This time I slowed the plane, called for "gear down," checked to be sure the trailing antenna was in, and turned on final. Over the threshold I eased off the power. The Lockheed bounced once lightly, but I didn't mind one bit! We were back! It was 1:43, local time. The flight had taken 18 hours and 25 minutes with an average groundspeed of about 135 mph. Two hours of fuel remained.

In front of the terminal were the people who had come to welcome us back. Hurriedly, we took our leis from the plastic bags and put them around our necks.

"Hurry up, Red Socks," said Payne. "They're waiting for you."

I crawled over the tanks, opened the door, and jumped into the bright California sunshine, a sea of welcoming faces, and a battery of microphones.

Soon my crew was standing beside me. Mr. Kilpatrick, who had given me an orchid when we had left, now placed a dozen red roses in my arms. I felt I was accepting them on behalf of another pilot who should have received them thirty years ago. An aide from Governor Reagan's office placed a carnation lei around my neck, adding to the Hawaiian ones.

Newsmen crowded around us. Question after question! We answered them as best we could. Then I met Vivian Maata who said, "I was Amelia's secretary prior to her final flight. She was a marvelous person and I admired her greatly. I would have been only too glad to welcome her back at this airport thirty years ago. Your plane, coming in today, could have been hers, and I feel a little sad. But, I congratulate you for completing the flight. It was a wonderful tribute."

Dr. Saidee Stark, who had been president of the Berkeley Zonta in 1937, and Mrs. Irene Hawks, the Area Director of Zonta, welcomed us as did Mr. Dimity, Mr. Aldridge from the Federal Aviation Administration, and Gordon Palmer who had been instrumental in getting a mountain named for Amelia and commemorative stamps issued in Surinam and Mali. Fred Goerner autographed copies of his book for Polhemus and me and had a long discussion with Polhemus.

AFTER LANDING at Oakland, July 7, 1967—California sunshine, a sea of smiling faces, and a battery of microphones. (Courtesy Port of Oakland)

In my room at the Edgewater West Motel were flowers from Ed Nagle, the manager, and roses from the Amelia Earhart Foundation. I returned a telephone call to Ted Graben from Saline, who had been aboard the Enterprise but could not get ashore in time to meet us at the airport. He came to the motel for a short visit and said the flight had been written up in the "Stars and Stripes."

Earl Koehler of Champion Spark Plug, was master of ceremonies at the dinner given by the company. Maxine Wood from J. Walter Thompson was the hostess. Among the hundred guests were John Reading, Mayor of Oakland; Ben Hutton, Executive Director of the Port of Oakland; Mr. Aldridge who gave us a telegram from General McKee, the head of the Federal Aviation Administration; Ted Holmes, tower chief at Oakland International; Mr. Dimity; and Doug Eaton and Fran Ortiz, the reporter and photographer who had met us a month ago. And so many others.

The surprise of the evening was a cake baked and decorated by Clayton Langehag, a bakery consultant staying at the motel. Roses and leaves trimmed the cake and along the lower edge were the words WELCOME ANN.

My crew and I each gave a short talk. More pictures were taken with the guests, and then there was a chance to visit. What a wonderful welcome it had been!

The following evening in Denver, Robert Stanley, a pilot during the Earhart search, and Ernest Humphrey, who had been assistant navigator at that time on the carrier Lexington which was used in the search, hosted us for dinner. Conversation flowed almost continuously with comparisons of the two flights.

That night I fell asleep thinking about 1937 and 1967. Tomorrow at Newton, Kansas, I would meet Muriel Morrissey, Amelia Earhart's sister.

NEWTON
OSHKOSH
WILLOW RUN

★
 ★
★

AT 3:00 ON SUNDAY, THE SHADOW of our Lockheed crossed the airport boundary at Newton, Kansas where Mrs. Morrissey, my husband, the wives of the crew members, and many others were waiting. Payne executed his runway-scraping fly-by and then I landed the plane. The flags on the sides of the taxiway rippled under a bright sun. As I swung the plane into position on the ramp, people began surging forward in spite of the policemen. Immediately, I cut the engines. The men in the temporary control tower said the people wanted me to stand up in the hatch. Lee slid back the bolts and I stood up.

So many people! I was overwhelmed. The band from Fort Riley played "Those Magnificent Men in Their Flying Machines." I waved at the sea of hands.

As I stepped from the plane, Don was the first to greet me, then Mrs. Morrissey. With her there was no formality. We slipped our arms around each other and it was as if we had been friends for a long time. Indeed this past month we had been especially close. Then Don, Mrs. Morrissey, and I walked to the cars waiting to take us to the speakers' stand.

These Kansans had begun arriving at noon for the buffalo barbeque and had watched sailplane demonstrations and parachute jumpers, listened to the band, seen exhibitions of the Phantom Drum and Bugle Corps, and taken airplane rides. Jean Coleman, general chairman of the Earhart Flight Commemoration at Newton, and John Bowers, manager of the Newton Chamber of Commerce, and the many who had helped

WITH MURIEL MORRISSEY, Amelia Earhart's sister, just after I landed at Newton, Kansas. (Courtesy Newton Kansan)

them had done a wonderful job. The atmosphere was almost Fourth of July, with only the fireworks missing.

When we had been seated on the speakers' platform, Representative Raymond King of Hesston, whose letter had started this welcome, introduced Mayor Lile Mason who gave me the key to the city of Newton. On behalf of Governor Docking, Gene Steuart and Dale McCollum of the Kansas Department of Economic Development presented me with a Kansas flag and paperweight. Then Garner Shriver, Representative to the U. S. Congress from Wichita, gave me a

United States flag which had been flown over the Capitol in Washington.

Mrs. Morrissey thanked me for completing the flight and said that Amelia would have liked me for a sister. As she pinned a silver four-leaf clover on my blouse, she commented, "For good luck, although you seemed to have had good luck all the way around and you're back safely."

What a lovely pin it was and how thoughtful of her to have given it to me. Amelia had indeed been fortunate to have her for a sister.

I gave Mrs. Morrissey a multi-colored leaf from the wreath, still bright with reds, yellows, and greens, and also one of the red roses given to me at Oakland.

Standing beneath the bright Kansas sun, I told the crowd about the high points of the flight, especially how we had found Howland Island. Then I introduced my crew and each in turn related his part in the flight.

Following this was a press conference in one of the hangars. About a dozen reporters were waiting, and an hour later most of their questions had been answered.

As we had flown around the world, our schedule had been hectic and I was disappointed not to have been able to meet other women who flew. Of course many of them had been in Washington for the International Convention of the Ninety-Nines. As I left the press conference, a woman beckoned. "We have some Ninety-Nines who would like to meet you."

In the main hangar were about thirty women pilots, many of whom had heard our broadcast into the Smithsonian. Now, ironically, I met these women from other countries in the middle of the United States. Shukria Ali I had especially wanted to meet, for in 1964 she had greeted Joan Merriman Smith who was flying the Earhart route in an Apache, when she had landed in Pakistan. There were women from India, the Netherlands, and ones from Australia who said that the captain of their jetliner had diverted so they could fly over Howland Island. We agreed that much improvement had been made in aircraft, navigation, and communication during the past thirty years.

That evening at the banquet I met the people from the

Newton area who had helped make this day a success. Among the many guests were Mayor and Mrs. Hazen Shaeffer of Atchison, Earhart's birthplace, and Velma Knearl, representing the Wichita Zonta which had sent me an autographed copy of "Courage Is the Price," Mrs. Morrissey's biography of Amelia.

After dinner Lee, Payne, Polhemus, and I answered more questions. Then Mrs. Morrissey spoke—such a youthful spirit she had, looking forward to the future but finding happiness in the present. "The flight," she said, "was a living tribute to Amelia, and I know she would have appreciated its completion."

She presented a copy of her book to the Newton Library and then, calmly and graciously, acknowledged a standing ovation. I thought about how much she had spoken in her sister's behalf for the past thirty years, and yet, how much a person she was in her own right.

Newton had given us a grand welcome—from the buffalo barbeque to the banquet. It had been a reunion for Don and me, for my crew and their wives, and a chance for us to meet Mrs. Morrissey.

The next morning the weather at Newton was perfect, but at Oshkosh, Lee's home town, it was not. Among all our charts and instrument approach plates, we had none for Oshkosh. An approach plate for Oshkosh was located and we drove several miles into the country to obtain it. The man who loaned it wanted it back—autographed by the four of us.

We took off at 7:30 local time on an instrument flight plan. As we neared Wisconsin, the clouds formed below us, necessitating an instrument approach.

At Oshkosh, Lee's relatives met us: parents, sisters, brothers, cousins, aunts, uncles, nieces, nephews. So many happy faces. All were proud of Lee and his Lockheed.

In the two hours we were there the sun broke through several times. We departed VFR (visual flight rules) for Detroit, but once across Lake Michigan, encountered a wall of ominous clouds which blocked our path. It had been raining in Michigan when we left; it was raining as we returned. Had the sun, I wondered, shone at all during our absence? After receiving an instrument clearance, I nosed the plane into the clouds. Rain cascaded down the windshield. The plane bounced in the air currents.

Fifty miles northwest of Willow Run we called Andrews Presidential and Liberty Airways and thanked them for their assistance, for being our voices away from home. Never again would "Rapid Rocket. Rapid Rocket" crackle over the headphones.

Cruising through the rain, I felt more alone than ever. The final leg of the world flight was almost over. I felt such a mixture of emotions—happiness to be returning combined with an undercurrent of regret that there would be no more new cities, no more joshing from my crew, no more engines droning hour after hour over endless oceans. The echoes of voices, those of people we had met, drifted through the cockpit.

When we were cleared for descent, I pointed the nose of that gallant Lockheed down and the plane moved swiftly through the gray mists. Radar vectored us onto final. Reducing power, I guided the Lockheed down the glide slope. Half a mile from the end of the runway the plane broke out of the overcast. In seconds white runway numbers flashed beneath the wings and the wheels touched, throwing spray as they rolled. Taxiing toward the hangar, I could see my parents, relatives, friends, and newsmen.

We were breaking up a family of five—the four of us and that grand old Lockheed. It had taken the cooperation and assistance of hundreds of people to get the Lockheed around the world. We had completed Amelia Earhart's flight plan from Oakland to Oakland, and now had finished ours. The right synthesis of plane, people, and flight plan had brought this venture to completion.

In front of the hangar I eased the mixture controls to idle cutoff for the last time. The propellers swung quietly and stopped. No one spoke. The cockpit was quiet except for the click of switches as Payne and I turned everything off.

I was remembering the preparations, the planning, and the days of the journey. We five had answered the call of distant horizons as another Lockheed 10, pilot, and navigator had done thirty years ago. For us, the world flight was complete.

EPILOGUE

FLYING AROUND THE WORLD was not a thought which had occurred to me—even in daydreams—long ago, but once the idea had taken root, it was hard to dislodge. Yet, if Lee had not rebuilt the Lockheed, if I had not met Bill Polhemus and Colonel Payne, and if hundreds of people had not helped, the flight would have remained a fanciful thought.

The Michigan Legislature declared July 15, 1967, "Ann Pellegreno Day." That same day was "Ann Day" in Saline where one of the longest parades in the city's history was staged. People lined the streets. "Ticker tape" rained from rooftops and a helicopter! My crew, their families, and Don and I were driven slowly down the main street. We waved. Hands and brightly colored welcome-back posters made by the children were waved in response.

Then we watched "our" parade from the reviewing stand. Over sixty units, many coming from neighboring towns and cities, filled the street with color, movement, and sound. Horses. Antique cars. Marching bands. Queens. Color guards. Such spirit! Such ingenuity! The floats used aviation motifs with the theme—"It's a Woman's World." On top of the water tower a large model airplane perched. A golden key, fully a foot long, to the city of Saline was given to me and my crew received individual plaques.

The names of all who participated in "Ann Day" would fill a book. To the people of Saline and surrounding communities who welcomed us back in such a fantastic way—a very special thank you to each of you!

EPILOGUE

At home hundreds of letters awaited replies. There were requests for autographs, speeches, personal appearances, information about the flight, interviews, radio and television shows! The article for "McCall's" and others for aviation magazines were written. The debt was enormous! Money owed immediately, not including that spent before the flight, was about $13,000. Don and I were completely broke—without even rent money. But, we agreed the flight had been worth it!

The next year and a half were the busiest of my life: flying the plane to several aviation gatherings, speeches—sometimes three a week—in different states, letters to be answered, telephone calls.

In March 1968 Lee sold the Lockheed to Air Canada, for-

FOUR CARLOADS of crew and families move slowly down the main street of Saline. (Courtesy Ann Arbor News)

"OUR" LOCKHEED, N79237, as it appears on permanent display in an annex to the terminal building at Ottawa International Airport. Once again it is registered as CF-TCA.

The two plaques, one in English and one in French, carry the same information. The one in English reads:

LOCKHEED "ELECTRA" 10A

The all-metal, twin-engine, ten passenger Lockheed Electra transport was first introduced in 1934 and immediately proved to be an excellent high speed passenger aircraft of the period. Regular Trans-Canada Airlines service began in 1937 with the type and CF-TCA, the first new aircraft to provide this service, is exhibited here in its original markings. After many years of useful service in North America, this historic aircraft was flown around the world in 1967 by Ann Pellegreno to commemorate the flight of Amelia Earhart thirty years before. It was subsequently acquired by Air Canada and presented to the National Aeronautical Collection.

Span	55 ft.
Length	38 ft. 7 inches
Weight (Loaded)	10,100 lbs.
Speed (Cruising)	195 miles per hour at 9,600 ft.
Engines	Two 400 h.p. Pratt and Whitney Wasp Juniors (Courtesy National Museums of Canada)

merly Trans-Canada, which had originally owned the plane. Dedicated men meticulously restored the plane to its 1937 configuration. In October of that year it was flown to Ottawa and presented to the National Museum of Science and Technology and put on permanent display in the annex of the terminal building at Ottawa International Airport. Two plaques in front of the plane, one in English and one in French, mention the world flight.

By November 1968 the flight debt had been paid and work was begun on this book.

Originally, Amelia Earhart's idea had been a world flight as near to the equator as possible, a flight to culminate her other records. Our flight was the completion of her original dream. She had written ''. . . failure must be but a challenge to others.'' We accepted her dream as a challenge, and desired to both commemorate and complete the 1937 endeavor thirty years later. Our flight was a unique synthesis of past, present, and future—a once-in-many-lifetimes adventure.

The satisfaction of having followed one ''Earhart trail'' to completion, however, drew my attention to another Earhart trail. The controversial hypotheses advanced to explain Earhart's disappearance have become a continuing interest.

PART TWO

THE EARHART CONTROVERSY

THIS SECTION will present some background to the 1937 flight and hypotheses relevant to the disappearance of Amelia Earhart. It seeks neither to evaluate these hypotheses nor to advance my own opinions. Since brevity is obviously necessary, a bibliography is provided.

The complete details of what occurred on that final leg of the 1937 flight may never become public knowledge. However, one fact stands— Amelia Earhart would have performed to the best of her ability what she undertook.

. . .

Since several hypotheses postulate Earhart's involvement in a U.S. intelligence mission, some background information concerning Japanese-American relationships prior to 1937 follows. After World War I, Japan received a mandate over the former German island possessions in the Pacific north of the equator and began a policy of discouraging foreign visits in Micronesia. These islands could be developed peaceably, but military fortifications were strictly forbidden.

Japan's continuing development as an aggressive power after 1894 was, to say the least, discomforting to nations bordering the Pacific. In terms of naval strategy there was growing concern about the constantly increasing Japanese military might. As the situation deteriorated, suspicions arose as to exactly what the Japanese had done and were doing in Micronesia—specifically regarding military operations. Had the islands been open for inspection, suspicions might have been allayed. By 1937 it seems likely that determining the extent of Japanese military installations in the mandated islands, assumed at the very least to be airfields and harbor facilities beyond commercial necessity, was of paramount concern to those in official and military circles in the United States.

. . .

In 1935 Pan American's China Clipper, piloted by Ed Musik and navigated by Fred Noonan, flew from San Francisco to Manila using island stops. Following this, commercial flights from Hawaii to Australia, again using island stopovers, were considered. The Bureau of Air Commerce consulted the State Department and found that Howland, Baker, and Jarvis Islands belonged to the United States. "Colonists," in the employ of the United States Army and serviced by the Coast Guard were settled on the three islands, the entire affair being conducted in secrecy. When the news broke, Japan suspected the United States of strategic subterfuge. By executive order on May 13, 1936, President Roosevelt placed the three islands under the control of the Secretary of the Department of the Interior. The United States also showed an interest in certain islands in the Phoenix group, located slightly more than 400 miles southeast of Howland.

. . .

There have been many inconsistencies in the data surrounding Earhart's Electra. Information from Lockheed, the Bureau of Air Commerce, people involved in the flight, and outside sources expresses conflicting views on the engines used, fuel tank capacity (listed from 1150 to 1202 gallons with several figures between, not to mention two different tank diagrams for NR16020), where and when equipment was installed, the airspeeds, and the range.

Various releases from Lockheed listed 2 Pratt and Whitney

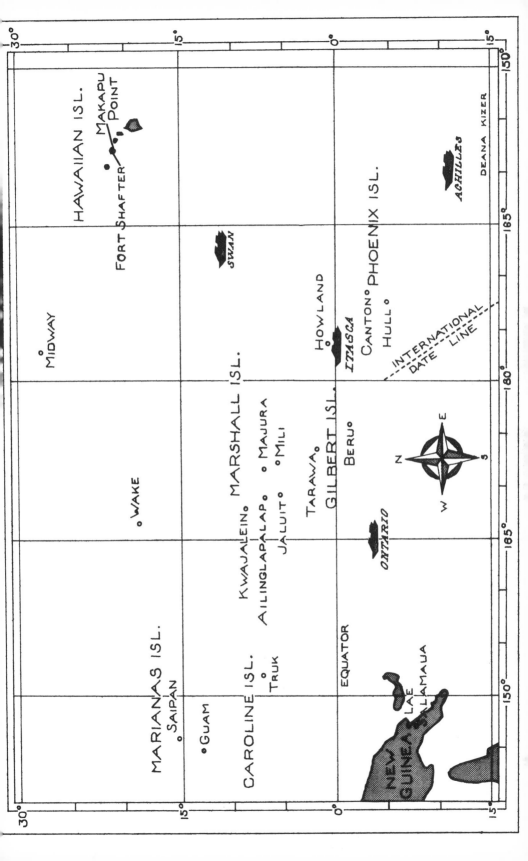

550 hp engines driving 2 Hamilton Standard propellers, a cruising range as both 4000 and 4500 miles, and a full overgross weight of 16,500 pounds. Special instruments, other than standard, included a Sperry Robot Pilot and a new type of fuel analyzer which would enable fuel consumption to be kept at a minimum under all flying conditions. Speed was listed as 202 mph maximum and 140 to 180 for maximum distance. The electrical generating system was a Leece Neville of added capacity to handle the navigation and communications gear.

After delivery, according to Lockheed, the plane had more work done on it at Union Air Terminal with Mantz and still more in Miami. This work included "installation of navigational and communications gear under the supervision of Fred Noonan (loaned from Pan Am for the mission). Extensive testing of fuel system operation and fuel consumption data was performed in the Southern California area along with calibration adjustment and modification to navigation and communication gear which (it was understood) was basically the Pan Am system of that day" (Lockheed Aircraft Corporation). This would be the equipment that Noonan had used when, during a survey flight in a Pan Am Clipper, he had hit Wake Island right on schedule.

Information about the Earhart stop at Lae came in two letters from James A. Collopy, who at that time (1937) had been District Superintendent of Civil Aviation in New Guinea. After Earhart's departure he had written a report of her stay which had gone into a file dealing with every aspect of her flight. About 1963 Collopy had obtained the file from the "Historical Flights" section of the department's records to answer questions for an Earhart researcher. However, when he tried to locate the file in 1967, it had "disappeared."

The first night at Lae, Amelia had had dinner with the Eric Chaters (manager of Guinea Airways) while Noonan, Collopy, and others had an enjoyable evening at the hotel. Collopy thought that the two fliers had differences of opinion but not "of such consequence to affect their operation." He noted that the next day and the night before take off were quiet. "Both were in bed early that night."

LOCKHEED ELECTRA R16020 showing painted cowlings, single window, and wingtip lights recessed from wingtip. (Courtesy Leo Kohn)

Guinea Airways mechanics, who had had prior experience with the 10E, worked on Earhart's plane. Fueling was done by Vacuum Oil. Collopy believes she took 900 gallons of standard aviation fuel, plus some high-octane fuel for take off which had been sent to Lae especially for her.

In summary, weather data compiled at Fleet Air Base at Honolulu from half a dozen stations (ships, islands, etc.) and sent to her at Lae indicated east southeast winds from 18 to 25 knots to the Ontario (stationed midway between Lae and Howland) and from there to Howland winds from the east northeast 15 to 20 knots. Heavy rain squalls were predicted in the area 300 miles east of Lae with scattered heavy showers and some cumulus buildups the remainder of the leg. (Weather from the Itasca indicated generally east winds at 11 mph.)

In "Last Flight," Earhart commented, "In addition, Fred Noonan has been unable, because of radio difficulties, to set his chronometers. Any lack of their fastness or slowness would defeat the accuracy of celestial navigation." Yet, the radio at Lae, used primarily for communications with other ground stations, was operating perfectly—the first-class operator receiving traffic for Earhart and monitoring her for seven and a half hours after her departure. Conceivably, Noonan could have received a time check through this facility. Considering the time taken to work on the plane at Bandoeng, ("Last Flight"; Itasca log) and the decision later made to

LAE STRIP at the time of Amelia Earhart's visit. (Courtesy Jim Collopy)

return to Bandoeng from Saurabaya because "certain further adjustments of faulty long-distance flying instruments were necessary" ("Last Flight"), it seems incredibly illogical that Noonan would have departed from Lae without the chronometers set accurately and the plane's radio working. Furthermore, the radio in the plane worked well during the early portion of the long hop to Howland.

Collopy wrote, "The take-off run was 3000 feet which was the total length of the runway and believe me she used it all. She bounced off at the very edge of the seaward end and dropped down to about 10 feet above the water and held it there in 'ground effect' for 3 to 5 miles before she pulled up to a very gentle climb."

LOCALITY PLAN.
Map of New Guinea & Papua   MILES

LAE.
at 26 2 35   YARDS

CLASS OF GROUND: Aerodrome suitable for all types of landplanes.
PROPRIETORS: Administration, Territory of New Guinea.
POSITION: At Lae, on coast, near the mouth of the Markham River.
   Lat. 6°48'S. Long. 147°2'E.
MAGNETIC VARIATION: 5½°E. approx.
DISTINCTIVE FEATURES: Sea on south, Lae Township in the north-
   east, Markham River, 1½ miles west.
MARKINGS: Nil.
DESCRIPTION: One way ground running north-west from coast.
DIMENSIONS: NW. - SE. 1000 yards by about 120 yards wide.
HEIGHT ABOVE SEA LEVEL: 25 ft. approx.
APPROACHES: South - east over sea.
           North - west over clearing with timber beyond.
SURROUNDING COUNTRY: Timbered with hills to the north-east.
PETROL AND OIL: At Lae.
WATER SUPPLY: Tanks on aerodrome.
WORKSHOPS: Guinea Airways, on Aerodrome.
HANGAR ACCOMMODATION: Limited space available in Guinea Airways
   Hangars.
TELEPHONE: Nil.
TELEGRAPH: Guinea Airway's private radio can communicate with
   Salamaua.
NEAREST TOWN: Lae.
NEAREST RAILWAY STATION: Nil.
CHARGES: Nil.
REMARKS: Normal winds - north-west during mornings and
                       south-east during afternoons.

a.a.mccomb

A/CONTROLLER OF CIVIL AVIATION.

S.363. P.617.

DATA on Lae Aerodrome at the time of Amelia Earhart's visit.
(Courtesy of Jim Collopy)

THE EARHART CONTROVERSY

Thus departed Amelia Earhart from Lae, New Guinea, accompanied by perhaps the world's most experienced aerial navigator, a veteran of more than a dozen trans-Pacific flights, in an airplane capable of flying in excess of 4000 miles.

Waiting at Howland Island, 2556 miles distant, were Commander Thompson and the crew of the Itasca who were to play an important but frustrating role. Aboard the ship also were Richard B. Black, Earhart's representative from the Department of the Interior and two news correspondents.

According to the ship's log, messages to Lae were routed via Tutuila, Suva, Sydney, Rabaul, and Salamaua, 14 miles south of Lae. Frequencies utilized in the vast Pacific radio network stretching from Manila to California, to Tutuila, and to Sydney ranged from 355 to 16,960 kilocycles. The Itasca and KFS, a coastal station in San Francisco 4000 miles away, were communicating on a call and answer basis using 12,600 kilocycles. Frequencies in the high frequency (HF) band, 3000 to 30,000 kilocycles are known for their amazing ability to travel as far as 12,000 miles.

Realizing that from a Coast Guard point of view the success or failure of communications depended upon the Itasca, Thompson sent his first direct message to Earhart on June 23 requesting her to advise the ship twelve hours before departing Lae and to indicate frequencies desired. As it occurred, Thompson spent the entire day of July 1 (July 2 at Lae) trying to ascertain if she had departed. Confirmation of her 10:00 a.m. Lae time (12:30 p.m. Howland time) departure was received from the Coast Guard at 7:00 p.m. on the Itasca.

A reading of the Itasca's radio log makes it apparent that the radio network in the Pacific was functioning properly, and it was ascertained that the Itasca's signals were heard throughout the Pacific.

According to Earhart's messages, the plane's direction finder covered from 200 to 1500 kilocycles and 2400 to 2800 kilocycles yet she asked that the Itasca transmit the letter "A" on 7500 kilocycles. Later she radioed that she understood the ship would be voicing on 3105 kilocycles with a long continuous signal on her approach. Discrepancies appear between her earlier and later messages.

Upon the arrival of the message stating Earhart had left Lae, a radioman second class was sent ashore to man the high frequency direction finder and two men were assigned radio watch on the ship. Two officers and two newsmen were also in the radio room on the Itasca. The message indicated an arrival at Howland in 18 hours, or at 6:30 a.m. Howland time, with an average groundspeed of 144 mph. The ship checked signal strength and frequency (3105 and 7500 kilocycles) using key and voice with San Francisco.

After Earhart was first heard at 2:45 a.m. saying "CLOUDY AND OVERCAST," the ship attempted further contact, but continued to send weather and homing signals using both code and voice on 3105 as well as 7500 kilocycles. Throughout the night the ship continually requested the plane's position, but the question was never answered.

At 3:45 Earhart broadcast, "ITASCA FROM EARHART . . . OVERCAST . . . WILL LISTEN ON HOUR AND HALF HOUR ON 3105 . . ."

At 4:53 she sent, "PARTLY CLOUDY." Two minutes later she came on again, but the message was unreadable. Volume level was S-1, the lowest.

At 6:14 she asked the ship to take a bearing on the plane and said she was about 200 miles out. Her whistling in the microphone was unsuitable and too brief for taking a bearing.

At 6:42 fairly clear signals calling the ship were received and at 6:45 she requested, "PLEASE TAKE BEARING ON US AND REPORT IN HALF HOUR I WILL MAKE NOISE IN MICROPHONE . . . ABOUT 100 MILES OUT"

The signal strength was S-4, almost the top reading, but she was on the air so briefly that taking a bearing was impossible.

At 7:42 she radioed, ". . . WE MUST BE ON YOU BUT CANNOT SEE YOU BUT GAS IS RUNNING LOW BEEN UNABLE REACH YOU BY RADIO WE ARE FLYING AT ALTITUDE ONE THOUSAND FEET"

At 7:58 she radioed, ". . . WE ARE CIRCLING BUT CANNOT HEAR YOU GO AHEAD ON 7500 EITHER NOW OR ON THE SCHEDULE TIME ON HALF HOUR"

The signal strength on that message was S-5, the highest. The only direct reply received from Earhart came at 8:00.

"... WE RECEIVED YOUR SIGNALS BUT UNABLE TO GET A MINIMUM PLEASE TAKE BEARING ON US AND ANSWER 3105 WITH VOICE"

At 8:44 she radioed, "WE ARE ON THE LINE OF POSITION 157-337 . . . WE WILL REPEAT THIS MESSAGE ON 6210 KILOCYCLES WAIT LISTENING ON 6210 KILOCYCLES"

Other people in the radio room heard, "WE ARE RUNNING NORTH AND SOUTH"

Nothing was heard on 6210 kilocycles. Men in the radio room agreed that the signal strength of the plane had remained about the same from 8:00 to 9:00 and that the last transmission had almost the same strength as the 7:58 one. Seven or eight seconds (insufficient to take a bearing) was estimated as the longest transmission received from the plane and toward the end Earhart had talked so rapidly as to be almost incoherent.

The smoke screen laid down by the ship stretched ten miles. At 10:15 the ship departed Howland to search the northwest quadrant where, 40 miles away a wall of clouds loomed, and where Thompson thought it most probable the plane had gone down. At 2:00 p.m. he sent a general message requesting ships and stations to listen for signals from the plane.

Both Mr. Putnam and Lockheed engineers felt the plane could float a considerable length of time due to the empty fuel tanks and stated a positive buoyancy of 5000 pounds with the plane weight at 8000 pounds. Until July 5 it was thought the plane could transmit if on water, but then radio technicians stated definitely the plane radio could not function unless the plane was on land and the right engine operable. However, it was reported that a spare battery was carried. Also, Mantz had considered the possibility of an off airport landing to the extent of inquiring about a twenty-pound emergency generator. It is uncertain, however, whether this generator was on board.

Numerous reports of hearing dashes and some voicing, mostly weak and unreadable, on 3105 and 6210 kilocycles came from ships, land-based military and commercial stations, and radio amateurs who were later (perhaps unfairly) condemned for reporting "false messages."

Fort Shafter in the Hawaiian Islands reported hearing a searching series of long dashes on 3105 kilocycles and again on 6210 kilocycles with weak voicing.

WKT, a coastal station in California, heard a fairly strong voice. However, the words were indistinguishable owing to either bad modulation or the speaker's shouting into the microphone. The voicing was similar to that emitted from the plane in flight with the exception that now there was no hum from the plane in the background.

Four Los Angeles radio amateurs reported hearing a position report from KHAQQ placing it west of Howland near the International Date Line.

The HMS Achilles, steaming about 1200 miles southeast of Howland reported that on 3105 kilocycles a telephone transmitter with a harsh note conveyed the message, "Please give us a few dashes if you get us." A second transmitter was then heard to make dashes and then the first transmitter made KHAQQ twice before fading.

Makapu Point PAA station on Oahu reported a true bearing of 213 degrees which could, due to a rough signal, be an approximation. Later a bearing taken on a stronger signal indicated 200 degrees true. On July 5 the PAA station on Wake Island reported a true bearing of 144 degrees. The Itasca asked PAA at Oahu and Wake to take a bearing check on the ship to determine the correction factor for the "Earhart bearings."

Confirmation never arrived.

Howland Island reported obtaining a bearing on a continuous wave on 3105 kilocycles with origin unknown indicating south southeast or north northwest from the island on a magnetic course.

On July 6, the Navy assumed the direction of the search and responsibility for monitoring 3105 kilocycles; the Itasca began operating under orders from the USS Colorado, steaming from Pearl Harbor, which would arrive in the search area on July 7. After refueling the Itasca, the battleship proceeded to the Phoenix Island area, launching its three catapult planes to search the islands, one plane landing off Hull Island. Reportedly, a resident there said no plane had been seen or heard. Its search completed by July 11, the Colorado refueled the Swan, and then proceeded north of Howland and after refueling the destroyers accompanying the carrier Lexington, returned to Hawaii. While the Itasca and Swan, now under orders from the carrier, searched the Gilbert Island area, the Lexington with its planes and destroyers searched an area west of Howland extending approximately to within 75 miles of the Gilberts; to the northwest the search extended to within 250 miles of the Marshall Islands.

. . .

The "Summary of the Search" in the Itasca radio log (dated July 23, 1937) included the following assertions:

"That the Earhart plane went down after 0846 July 2nd and apparently sent no distress message.

"That amateurs reported several messages, all probably criminally false, but that Pan American, Howland, and other stations had taken bearings on a carrier (wave) someplace in the Pacific."

"That Itasca signals calling Earhart, the March of Time program, and other signals were interpreted as being from Earhart."

"That all available land areas were searched; therefore the plane was not on land."

"That the Itasca's original estimate after three weeks of search still appeared correct—that the plane went down to the northwest of Howland."

"That in time opinions on the Earhart flight and its communications will be definitely formulated."

. . .

The "Report of the Earhart Search" USS Lexington concludes:

"Although unfortunately the fate of the missing fliers remains a mystery, it is considered that the search made was efficient and that the areas covered were the most probable ones, based on all the facts and information available."

The government and military have maintained that Earhart went down at sea near Howland. The following hypotheses agree with that reasoning.

. . .

In "Courage Is the Price" (1963) Mrs. Morrissey discusses her own beliefs concerning what happened to her sister as well as the hypotheses of others. She notes, "If the Electra had been forced down over Saipan or the Marshalls, it would indicate a severe navigational error." A noted woman pilot, who was given a final mission by General "Hap" Arnold to make an official investigation into the activities of Japanese women in the Imperial Air Force, found information on several American fliers, including Amelia Earhart, in Japanese government files which were then supposed to have been sent to Washington for microfilming. As the file was still "open" in 1945, Mrs. Morrissey wrote that it "seems unlikely that the Japanese government had any knowledge of her being 'liquidated' by their orders. The lack of official notation of the capture of so well-known a figure by any Japanese military or civilian personnel seems to vitiate this theory of the disappearance of the Electra's crew." And as to Amelia being a spy—"No word of such a mission is to be found in the writing of either the former President or Amelia."

Returning servicemen have told Mrs. Morrissey of talking either directly with English-speaking natives or through translators with others on Pacific Islands who knew about the white woman and man fliers. One man told her that he had talked with a woman whom he later thought might have been Amelia, but his efforts to relocate the fishing village where he had the conversation have not been fruitful.

Although many conflicting reports have come to Mrs. Morrissey through the years, she concludes, ". . . I agree with

Commander Thompson's theory that Amelia's plane was submerged within a hundred miles of Howland Island."

. . .

In "Hollywood Pilot" (1967) by Don Dwiggins it is unmistakably affirmed that Paul Mantz, Earhart's $100-a-day technical advisor, believed that she went down at sea near Howland. He had set up Amelia's radio schedule for the 1935 Honolulu to Oakland flight, and had at that time flown her red Vega 12,000 feet over Diamond Head and talked with KFI in Los Angeles. Halfway between Honolulu and Oakland, Earhart was coming in loud and clear at that station.

Mantz supervised the preparation of the Electra and coached Amelia on instrument flying. A Sperry Robot Pilot was advocated to eliminate half the fatigue associated with long-distance flying and Clarence Belinn, superintendent of engineering for National Airways, was asked to design a foolproof fuel system. Three tanks were put in each wing root and six additional tanks in the fuselage between the cockpit and the navigation desk. Total gallonage was 1202. (Tank diagram appears in "Hollywood Pilot.")

During the flight to Honolulu on the first world attempt in March 1937, Earhart and Mantz sat in the cockpit and Harry Manning and Fred Noonan in the chart room to check the navigation techniques they had worked out. Mantz had been particularly pleased with Noonan's work, his efficiency, and his refined technique gained from working as a master mariner and from navigating trans-Pacific Clippers for Pan American.

Mantz had worked out power curves for the long flights, recommending 28 inches of manifold pressure and 1900 rpm for the first three hours at 8000 feet. This was practically wide-open flying and the reading on the Electra's Cambridge fuel analyzer was .78, meaning fuel consumption was 60 gallons per hour. As fuel was burned, progressively lower settings were called for until an estimated 38 gallons per hour were being burned, and a true airspeed of 150 mph being maintained.

Mantz was pleased with Amelia's flying on this flight of some 2400 miles for she held to compass headings reasonably well, and when straying off a degree or so, properly corrected to bring the plane back on course. When Noonan asked her to hold Makapu Point beacon "ten degrees on the starboard bow," she maintained a heading which held the needle on the radio compass ten degrees to the right—the drift correction Noonan had calculated. At that time the Electra was more than 100 miles from Honolulu and the loop antenna had worked perfectly. However, when Manning held the key down so the Makapu Point directing finder could pick up a "null" on the plane, the generator burned out.

During the night of July 2, 1937, Mantz had monitored her transmissions, maintaining a vigil at KFI, hoping for confirmation of a safe arrival at Howland. He was furious because she had left her trailing antenna behind, thus reducing the distance at which 500 kilocycles would be effective. Later, Mantz thought the Electra had been unquestionably close to Howland as Earhart's voice (as noted in the Itasca log which he received after the flight) had grown from a weak volume to full strength. He also wondered why the radio stations at Tarawa and Beru in the Gilberts had not been notified since the announced flight path lay over the southern end of that island group.

. . .

Robert Stanley, a naval aviation cadet in 1937, participated in the Earhart search as a pilot aboard the carrier Lexington. After delays involving provisioning, fueling, aircraft, and personnel, the carrier finally left Honolulu at 3:15 p.m. on July 9 (almost a week after the ship had been first notified at Santa Barbara, California) and arrived in the Howland area on July 13. Stanley was "volunteered" to be cartographer for the search. The only chart of that area of the Pacific aboard the carrier was in a dog-eared 1841 whaling book showing islands reported at one place in 1776 and five or ten miles away in 1820. Stanley thought that sending a carrier of that value to virtually uncharted waters at those speeds (30 to 35 knots when launching planes) bordered on the foolhardy. During the search he flew over areas where the 1841 whaling book indicated shoals and little atolls and saw nothing.

He recalls that rain squalls covered only about one percent of the search area—but that one percent was important if the objects of the search were beneath the rains. Stanley also felt that from an altitude of 700 feet with one-half mile search responsibility on each side, the raft or plane might have been missed due to the roughness of the seas.

For six days aircraft searched a total of 151,556 square miles of Pacific Ocean and the carrier and three accompanying destroyers another 22,640 square miles with negative results.

Stanley, president of Stanley Aviation Corporation, still believes that Amelia Earhart could not see Howland or the Itasca because of squalls to the northwest and went down within 100 miles of Howland.

. . .

In a report titled, "Howland Island: ETA Thirty Years and Thirty Minutes," Bill Polhemus compares the 1937 and 1967 flights as to radio gear, fuel management, airplane performance, and navigation equipment and procedures. He feels his analysis should "leave the thoughtful reader with an explanation for Earhart's disappearance which, while less dramatic than some of those presently before the public, is infinitely more plausible."

He believes Noonan should have experienced no difficulty with the en route navigation and estimates that the plane's 6:15 a.m. Howland time position (200 miles out) was accurate to "not worse than 20 nautical miles" which, considering the estimated time of arrival, would have made the sun line landfall technique ideal. It is also assumed that Noonan knew his true airspeed to within 2 or three knots. Hence, his position at at 7:58 (100 miles out) when the signal strength was also strongest would not have been more than 40 nautical miles from Howland. Even if Noonan had not known exactly what the correct azimuth of the sun was at the two aforementioned times, the small error would not have accounted for being unable to locate the island. However had the plane been in the northwest quadrant, storm clouds might have made it impossible for Earhart to see either the island or the smoke screen laid by the Itasca.

After 7:30 a.m. Noonan could no longer shoot a star fix— perhaps his most accurate method of determining position. Assuming that Noonan had made a 30-degree turn off course to intercept the sun line 60 miles northwest of the island, the turn would have been to 157 degrees at about 8:00 a.m. at which time the correct course would have been 153 degrees. With a 30-minute run-in to Howland and no error in heading, the plane should have passed Howland 4 miles to the west. Polhemus feels Noonan's heading could have erred by 2 or 3 degrees at most during the inbound flight, an error too small to have caused them to miss the island.

During the night, Nauru Radio had heard six transmissions from the plane, including the last two sent to Lae Radio. The 10:30 Zulu (11:00 p.m. Howland time) report was "A ship in sight ahead," and was heard on 3105 kilocycles (the Ontario was positioned midway between Lae and Howland). On the basis of that, her position was probably near 2 degrees 59 minutes south and 165 degrees and 6 minutes east, and consequently near where the Ontario was stationed. However, merchant vessels also could have been on the flight path. An hour later her last position report was received by Nauru.

Polhemus noted that Earhart's last transmission was heard in the Howland area with good signal strength on 3105 kilocycles at 8:55 a.m., but was interrupted in the middle. Further transmissions that morning were heard by Nauru Radio at 9:01, 9:03, and 9:24 on 6210 kilocycles, the plane's daylight frequency. However, Nauru Radio later reported, "Speech not interpreted owing bad modulation or operator shouting into the microphone but voice similar to that emitted in flight last night with exception of no hum of plane in background." (Reference for Nauru Radio information used in the Polhemus report is "Amelia Earhart's Last Flight: A Tragedy of Errors" compiled by Captain L. F. Safford, USN, Retired.)

Based on his estimate of fuel aboard at Lae (900 gallons) and of fuel expended during flight, Polhemus calculates 9:20 a.m. Howland time for dry tanks. He believes Earhart was on a direct flight from Lae and concludes the report, "It is my opinion that the aircraft did go down in the vicinity of Howland Island and that the proximate cause was the inability or failure to properly complete the landfall technique once it was initiated."

. . .

The Lockheed 10 is a rugged airplane, the main wing spar extending through the fuselage. In promotional literature issued in the 1930s by Lockheed, item 12 on a sheet titled "Electra Highlights" reads: "Has been landed with wheels retracted with a full load of passengers as demonstration of safety." Consequently, even if Earhart went down on land instead of at sea, there is a decided possibility that the crash was not fatal. If she went down at sea, the crash also would not necessarily have been fatal. To illustrate this point, in August 1967, the pilot of a Lockheed 10E experienced engine failure of the right engine. Shortly thereafter the left engine lost power. Unable to maintain altitude, the pilot landed the plane on the water into a ten-mile-per-hour wind just off the Massachusetts coast with the left engine still running. Thirteen passengers and the pilot exited from either the hatch above the cockpit or the fuselage door and later it was estimated that the plane had floated for eight minutes. One witness on shore noted that the tail had been lowered just prior to contacting the water, an attitude which would allow the easiest deceleration. Passengers stated that the touchdown had been smooth and individual injuries were limited to strains and bruises.

In the Howland Island area on the morning of July 2, 1937, the wind was less than 10 mph from the east, the visibility was

20 miles, and wave action was a calm swell from an easterly direction.

. . .

Although the disappearance-at-sea rationale has been insisted upon by the government and the military, contrary explanations have persisted.

As early as December 1939, "Popular Aviation" published an article titled Is Amelia Earhart Still Alive? which began with the edict issued by Superior Judge Elliot Craig on January 5, 1939, five and a half years before Amelia Earhart could be declared legally dead. "With all the evidence before me," he said, "I can reach no other decision. Amelia Earhart Putnam died on or about July 2, 1937. . . ." Illustrative material in the article was supplied by Mr. Putnam from a portion of the thousands of "deeply moving appeals" he had received from a wide variety of people.

In November 1942, "Skyways" published an article titled The War's First Casualty, written by Charles Palmer, an "associate of George Palmer Putnam who is now with the armed forces." Although the article conceded it probable that the two fliers had perished in the waters of the South Pacific or crashed on one of the tiny islands, the author felt there was something "irresistibly irregular" about the story and that certain elements were missing or contradictory. He looked askance at the details of financing the flight; suggested that the Japanese could have discovered the scheme to fly over the mandated islands; declared that the search by the Navy was used to advantage to penetrate the forbidden islands; pointed to the "lack" of government involvement apparent in the building of an airstrip and the stationing of ships as plane guards at Howland and midway between Lae and Howland as well as Howland and Honolulu; and noted Earhart's refusal to radio her position to the Itasca. While no definite conclusion was reached, the author felt facts indicated that "aviation's greatest mystery was preempted by something more than a 'fatal piece of foolishness.' "

. . .

On Saipan in the early part of July 1944 Army Technical Sergeant Thomas E. Devine accidentally became involved with the Earhart mystery which he feels is one of the best kept secrets of World War II.

One morning his commanding officer ordered Devine to drive him to the captured Aslito Airfield which was within view of their bivouac area. When they approached what appeared to be an administration building adjacent to an intact hangar, a group of officers was discussing the Amelia Earhart plane which some officers said was inside the padlocked hangar now guarded by Marines. One guard asked Devine to remove his jeep from the roadside at the other end of the hangar. Devine queried him about the Earhart plane being in the hangar.

"I don't know why they want to keep it a secret," the guard said. "Of course it's in there, but don't say I told you."

Back at Devine's bivouac area, a Marine who had been on guard duty at the field stopped at the area to bid adieu to an army sergeant from his home town and mentioned the airplane and that Aslito Field was now off limits to everyone, even the Marine guards because Earhart's plane was to be flown. When Devine questioned him further, the Marine said he was not supposed to say anything and changed the subject to bracelets made of metal from Japanese planes.

Early in the afternoon two single-engine American military planes approached over Devine's encampment and landed at Aslito. An hour later, sounds emanated from the vicinity of the airport—the noise of engines revving up and then idling for some time, followed by a loud roar as if an airplane were taking off. Silence followed. Perhaps ten minutes later a twin-engine double-tailed civilian plane with the number NR16020 approached from the south flying over the encampment area and then landed.

That evening Devine and another soldier went over to the airfield, seeking aluminum for souvenir bracelets. In front of a battered hangar which was a short distance from the intact hangar where Devine had taken his commanding officer, was a twin-engine double-tailed plane with no military markings. As Devine approached, a man photographing the plane ran in the opposite direction. On the airfield was a single-engine fighter type plane with its engine idling and in the distance was another of the same type with someone standing beside it

Turning his attention to the civilian plane, Devine noted the twin-tail with NR16020 painted on it. However, not being familiar with aircraft registrations, he never realized that "N" meant United States registry and the "R" meant restricted. Riveted metal squares were where windows ordinarily would have been, the left tire had gone flat, and one word on the propeller was Hamilton. (Hamilton Standard propellers are used on Lockheed 10's.) Since he had come to obtain aluminum for a bracelet, and the aluminum on this airplane wasn't shiny, he deduced it was not Japanese and turned his attention to some nearby Japanese material. As his buddy was attempting to climb up on the right wing, they noticed the photographer had returned and was bringing his camera down from eye level, evidently having taken their picture. However, again he ran away. Two men, one with a bandolier of ammunition over his shoulder, were leaving the intact hangar and walking toward the idling airplane. The photographer waved them back. They returned. Since it was getting dark, Devine and his buddy returned to their area, looking backwards at one of the men who was noting their departure.

Half an hour later Devine heard an explosion. Seeing a fire at the airfield, he walked to the field perimeter. The civilian airplane was engulfed in flames. Soon two single-engine planes roared over him.

About a year later a group of soldiers, including Devine, paused near a small cemetery on Saipan. A native woman started talking rapidly and pointing to the ground. A translator said she was telling of two white people, one a woman, who had come from the sky and were buried nearby. At the time Devine thought the woman may have been demented or shocked by the bombardment, but later realized that her gestures may have meant a short-haired woman or perhaps decapitation.

Devine surmises that when the line of position 157-337 was

given, the plane was in the area west northwest of the Marshalls with ample fuel to reach Saipan. He does not believe that the two were on an intelligence mission, but that Noonan, after calculating their position simply headed for the nearest and largest United States territory—Guam. However, by error or prior knowledge, Noonan guided the aircraft on a landing field on Japanese-held Saipan, only 115 miles north of Guam.

In his continuing efforts to verify facts and learn what happened to Amelia Earhart, Devine has traveled to Saipan, talked with many people involved in some way with Earhart or her airplane, been confronted with governmental and military "closed doors," found that certain documents are "missing," and that information he has given the military is returned in blurred, unreadable form when requested by a second party. Devine has had occasion to believe that he was under surveillance.

It is his contention that the attempt to conceal the identity of the Earhart plane on Saipan was an intelligence mission instituted by the top authority of a war-time government. In spite of much that has been printed which Devine feels verges on hoax, his quest continues to learn the truth and make relevant the events witnessed on Saipan in 1944 and 1945.

. . .

In his biography of Amelia Earhart, "Daughter of the Sky," Paul Briand, Jr. relates the tale of Josephine Blanco.

In 1946 she was working as an assistant to an American dentist on Saipan and overheard a discussion with a patient as to whether Amelia Earhart might have gone down in the Marianas. Josephine told the dentist she had seen an American woman flier.

In 1937 eleven-year-old Josephine had been taking lunch to her brother-in-law who worked in the restricted area near Tanapag Harbor. She had a special pass into the area where not even Japanese civilians were admitted unless they carried the proper credentials.

A silver two-engine plane, apparently in trouble, landed in

the vicinity of the harbor. Josephine saw a man and a woman referred to as the "American woman," who wore a shirt and trousers and had short hair like a man. The two Americans were led away by Japanese soldiers. Shots were heard and the soldiers returned alone.

After seeing a photograph of Amelia Earhart and Fred Noonan, Josephine Blanco, now Mrs. Akiyama, confirmed that the couple were the same ones who had been led away.

In a letter to this author dated July 10, 1967, Paul Briand wrote:

> As far as I am concerned, there is no question whatsoever that she and Fred ended up on Saipan, and, I think by accident after getting lost, but they were mistaken as spies and executed as such, sooner or later either on Saipan, in Tokyo, or elsewhere. I don't think there are any simple answers, like she went into the drink somewhere around the Marshalls.

.   .   .

In 1960, Fred Goerner, author of "The Search for Amelia Earhart" (1966), became intrigued with the mystery after reading a clipping which told of a Mrs. Akiyama, who, on Saipan in 1937, had seen two American fliers, a man and a woman.

In the six years prior to publication of his book, Goerner as a CBS newsman made four trips to Saipan and scoured the United States for leads and information relating to the disappearance of the famous woman pilot.

On the first trip, the commander of the Naval Administration Unit on Saipan identified six men who would know something if anyone did and insisted that Goerner interview them initially. The men had had strong ties with the Japanese in 1937 or were currently working for the Navy on the island. Although they replied negatively to Goerner's questions, he felt their reticence in discussing the subject. On a subsequent trip, one of the men told Goerner that the woman flyer and a man accompanying her had been picked up in the Marshall Islands, brought to Saipan, and possibly had not left the island.

With the assistance of the Catholic priests on Saipan, more than 200 people were interviewed. From their testimonies Goerner felt that either Earhart and Noonan or persons closely resembling them had been on Saipan in 1937. After interrogation at Japanese military police headquarters in Garapan City, the woman had been taken to prison for a few hours, and then to the hotel in Garapan City which housed political prisoners. None of the people interviewed knew exactly what had happened to the man and woman, but several thought it possible that one or both had been executed.

Gregorio Camacho had seen the white man and woman at Tanapag Harbor and later in Garapan City. Jesus Boyer saw them at Tanapag Harbor and remembered the woman's short haircut. Jesus Salas, a prisoner in the Garapan prison in 1937, recalled that a white woman, whose description fit that of the other witnesses, had been placed in a cell next to him for a few hours. Josepa Reyes Sablan had seen the white fliers taken into the military police headquarters in Garapan City. Manual Aldan, a native dentist in 1937, reported that his Japanese officer patients often referred to the white woman flier. Before the war a Japanese soldier had shown Remedios Jons and her sister an unmarked grave of an American man and woman who had been fliers and killed as spies.

Mrs. Joaquina Cabrera had done laundry for the Japanese and their prisoners who stayed in the hotel in Garapan City. She described a man who had worn a bandage around his head and a woman wearing pants and a jacket, who appeared thin and tired-looking, and who had been questioned daily by the Japanese. Perhaps a year later, the police told Mrs. Cabrera that the woman was "dead of disease."

After two interviews during which he had remained sullen and uncooperative, a Saipanese who had worked with the Japanese military police before and during the war finally told Goerner that the Japanese had captured the white woman flier and her companion far away and brought them to Saipan. He admitted knowing where they were buried, but denied having anything to do with their deaths.

Goerner learned that the Japanese had begun construction of their naval seaplane base at Tanapag Harbor in 1929 and that by the mid-thirties civilian and military flights were coming and going from Japan and the mandated islands. (He has since found that Aslito Field, the Japanese fighter-bomber base at the southern end of the island, was operational in 1937.)

After the Allied invasion of 1944, two native brothers on Majuro Atoll in the Marshalls told of the American fliers, a man and a woman, whom the Japanese had picked up in 1937 and taken together with some of their equipment to another island. This report was later confirmed by a Lieutenant Bogan who did not doubt that Earhart had landed in the Marshalls and had even reported this to his superior officer who said he would not send the information to the States as it might raise false hopes that Earhart was alive.

A native named Elieu who taught school, said that Ajima, a trader, had told of a white woman flier who had run out of gas and landed between Jaluit and Alingalapap. Bogan found it hard to believe the men were telling anything but the truth for the Micronesians had been virtually without communications with the outside world since the Japanese had taken over the islands. Articles published in the United States relating Bogan's information had been written by Eugene Burns, an AP correspondent on Majuro in 1944. Two other American men in the Marshalls had been convinced that Elieu told the truth. One man was convinced the Japanese had captured Earhart and Eugene Burns's widow said her husband had spoken of returning to the Marshalls to follow the Earhart Trail.

After the invasion of the Marshalls, a Marine told of finding a suitcase in a barracks room which had been fitted up for a woman. In the suitcase were a number of clippings on Amelia Earhart, some woman's clothing, and a locked diary with the words "10-year Diary of Amelia Earhart." Another Marine had talked with natives who said that in 1937 a white woman and man were in the Kwajalein Atoll area for a short time before being taken to another island.

Goerner received a letter from a man who had been on Saipan in 1944 and had seen snapshots of Earhart. One possessed by a Japanese prisoner showed her near some

Japanese aircraft. Although the photograph was forwarded through intelligence channels, no trace of it can be found today. A Marine who had been on Saipan in 1944 reported seeing a photograph showing Earhart standing in an open field with a Japanese soldier.

While serving on Saipan as an interpreter, a Seabee heard native stories about Japanese bragging before the war of capturing "some white people" and bringing them to Saipan where they were "buried near a native cemetery."

Everett Hensen and Billy Burks who had been Marine PFC's on Saipan in 1944 related that under the direction of a Marine captain named Griswold, they had excavated a grave containing two skeletons just outside the small cemetery of Garapan City. When Hensen had inquired whose remains they were, Griswold had replied, "Did you ever hear of Amelia Earhart?" and then admonished the men to keep quiet.

To date Griswold does not remember ordering the excavation and the Marine Corps has neither confirmed nor denied the allegation.

Goerner interviewed a man who said he had signed an oath in 1937 not to reveal information about the Electra. Among other things, however, he did admit in response to a direct question that the plane was capable of flying over the Carolines and the Marshalls en route to Howland. Although refusing to name others who had worked on the plane, he suggested talking with men who had been at Hamilton Army Air Base in northern California during 1937.

During the course of his investigation, Goerner talked with the secretaries employed by Earhart in California, radiomen from the Itasca, the military services and their related intelligence branches, and "official" Washington.

The book concludes that after overflying Truk, Earhart encountered stormy weather and headwinds stronger than anticipated. When Howland did not appear, she had turned toward the Marshalls and landed offshore at Mili Atoll. Noonan injured his head during the landing. Distress signals were sent with an emergency radio. Eventually, a Japanese ship took them to Jaluit, Kwajalein, and finally Saipan.

. . .

In a letter dated April 21, 1971 to this author, Goerner wrote that information now available relative to the radio messages during the 1937 flight and data on the Electra have caused him to change his thinking "with respect to the possibility that Amelia Earhart was herself taking part in an overflight mission of the Japanese mandates."

.   .   .

"Amelia Earhart Returns from Saipan" (1969) by Joe Davidson chronicles the trips a group of men from the Cleveland area made to Saipan in 1967 and 1968 in an attempt to investigate the non-military plane without engines which one of the men, Donald Kothera, had seen in a box canyon on that island in 1946. No damage had been visible, so the plane could not have landed there. The jungle which had grown up around it indicated it had been there for a few years. Kothera thought it strange that the interior contained no seats, nets, or racks, and that no bullet holes were apparent. After World War II Kothera still wondered about that airplane, and occasionally looked at a picture of it. (No picture of the plane appears in the book, however.)

On the first expedition the canyon was located, but only a few parts of the plane remained. These were brought back and analysis established that the aluminum was of a type produced by Alcoa prior to 1937.

On Saipan the second time, the men took photographs of and taped interviews with people who recollected seeing either Amelia Earhart or Fred Noonan or the airplane.

Men from the Central Intelligence Agency and the Navy had come to Saipan several times since 1957, done some excavating, questioned people specifically about Amelia Earhart, and cautioned them to "remember nothing." Understandably, some people were reluctant to talk with the Cleveland group even though it seemed apparent they knew something. Some said they knew nothing, and still others suggested talking to another person who would know.

Strangely enough, a man from the United States who said he was vacationing on Saipan, seemed either to be tailing the

Cleveland group or one jump ahead of them for he turned up again and again and seemed especially interested in their activities.

However, some people on the island volunteered information, in fact, some of the same ones with whom Goerner had talked.

Joaquine Cabrera had seen an American woman riding in a motorcycle sidecar in 1937.

The Chief of Police on Saipan in 1968 was certain that Amelia had been there in 1937 and said that his two predecessors had denied any knowledge of the fliers until two years after the United States had occupied the island. Then both had admitted her presence.

Matilde San Nicolas, 24 years old in 1937, had lived in Garapan behind the Kobayashi Royokan Hotel where political prisoners were housed. (This woman in Goerner's book said a white lady had written something on a map of the Pacific in her geography book.) Mrs. San Nicolas remembered the white woman who had been kept under constant guard and, after seeing pictures of Amelia Earhart, was certain the woman had been the famous flier. Matilde's mother, who had learned English on Guam, had talked with the woman often. The lady had become progressively weaker, it was thought from dysentery, and had given Matilde's sister a white gold ring with a pearl in the center. Then the white woman had disappeared.

Louis Igatol and his friend Joe Blass, while at work at Tanapag Harbor, remembered seeing the white woman flier exit from the rear seat of a car with a Japanese admiral. Igatol recalled her being thin with short hair and the only white person he had seen during the times before the war. At that time he said the Japanese military were already on Saipan.

Anthony Diaz, a truck driver in 1937, said he had been called inside the restricted Japanese seaplane base at Tanapag Harbor to help build a road into the jungle to bring out an airplane. There were no airstrips on Saipan at that time and the plane had apparently landed on the beach and slid into some pinelike trees, sustaining very little damage, if any. Diaz said he had seen a man and a woman wearing jacket and pants, both of whom the Japanese foreman indicated were Americans. The plane, Diaz was told, eventually had been loaded on a ship and sent to Japan. When shown a picture of Earhart's plane, Diaz identified it as similar to the plane he had seen.

Anna Magofa, the daughter of Antonio Diaz, who had been seven years old in 1937, told of being on her way home from school and seeing two Japanese watching a white man and woman digging a hole just outside the cemetery near Garapan City. The Japanese then blindfolded the man, forced him to kneel, and beheaded him. This traumatic sight gave Anna nightmares for years. However, she also realized that the tall man with the large nose did not look as mean as Japanese propaganda depicted Americans.

She accompanied the Cleveland group to that spot, locating the old road, the ruins of the old crematorium, and then told them to dig about ten paces from the large forked breadfruit tree. The men screened an area of about six cubic feet, and found bone fragments, a three-tooth gold bridge, and some evidence that the grave had previously been exhumed.

After returning to the States, the men gave the bone fragments and bridge to an anthropologist whose general conclusion was that the cremated bones were "those of a female, probably white individual, between the anatomical ages of 40 to 42" and the single unburnt bone was not associated with the cremated remains, but "the remains of a second individual, a male."

Attempts to locate specific information about Amelia Earhart in Washington, D.C. were fruitless. The State Department admitted possession of a classified file, but refused to declassify it. Letters sent to Japan were answered— with the exception of those mentioning Amelia Earhart.

The Cleveland group believe that top level civilian and military authorities visited Earhart prior to her second world flight and that the United States government knew or knows more than it is willing to reveal. Therefore, the final solution, they feel, now hinges upon the decision of someone in the government to talk or upon a Marine captain named Griswold's remembering exhuming the grave on Saipan and the disposition of the remains.

. . .

Joe Klaas, the author of "Amelia Earhart Lives" (1970) introduces a woman who strongly resembles Amelia Earhart, walks like her, talks like her, but claims she is not the missing flier. A man, whom the author contends resembles Fred Noonan in appearance, stance, and career, denies, likewise, that he is Noonan. With leading characters like these, the reader is plunged into a tale surrounded by more than thirty years of intrigue.

The book, based on "Operation Earhart," begun by Joe Gervais in 1960, details visits with people who recalled seeing a woman flier on Saipan, but did not witness an execution or burial. Photographs and explanations intimate there may have been as many as five planes involved in the Earhart flight. Gervais investigated a Lockheed listed in files as a 12A, which, carrying Earhart's registration number, N16020, crashed and burned on a mountainside in 1961.

Gervais hypothesized that Earhart overflew Truk and the Marshalls, and was then to "get lost" by landing on the 6000-foot runway on Canton Island, so that the Navy could search for her over the mandated islands. However, something happened—did the Japanese force her down and then pluck her off Hull Island which lies 157 degrees true from Howland? A filmstrip taken at Hull Island and later released by the Navy, shows what could be a Japanese flag and the wreck of an airplane on the beach when the frames are viewed individually.

At a luncheon on Long Island in 1965, Gervais met a woman who was wearing a miniature major's oak-leaf cluster and an enameled miniature metal replica of the red, white, and blue ribbon which can only be worn by those who have been presented with the American Distinguished Flying Cross. The woman admitted she had flown with Amelia Earhart quite a lot, was a member of the Ninety-Nines and Zonta, but appeared apprehensive when Gervais snapped her picture. Although the woman and her husband did not remain for Gervais's lecture, she called him later, inviting him and his wife to dinner the following evening. Gervais took a raincheck because of previously made plans.

When he tried to collect that raincheck, the woman agreed to meet him in Montreal, but never arrived. During a later telephone conversation she asked Gervais exactly what he wanted to talk to her about. He said that when the names of eight Phoenix Islands are put in a certain order, and letters crossed out a particular way, the name of her husband appears and that the numerical sequence of the letters in his name designates the exact longitude and latitude of Hull Island. After saying, "Oh that. . . ." the woman asked Gervais to put into writing exactly what he wanted to know. The first letter was answered; the second was not.

Gervais surmised that Earhart spent the war years in the Imperial Palace in Japan, leaving that country shortly after the war. The price for her release—the assurance that the Emperor would not be tried as a war criminal and would remain in power—were concessions severely criticized by our allies who opted for unconditional surrender.

The book concludes with one certainty: "Joe Gervais is on your trail, Amelia. There's no use trying to die, for he'll follow you wherever you go, and as long as he shall live, you shall live."

.   .   .

For all the hypotheses to be true would be an impossibility. Yet, none has withstood cross examination and unanswered questions remain. The steadfast refusal of the government and the military to open all its files has spurred ever more persistent speculation, and material contradicting official statements continually appears.

However, even if it is granted that speculation could be arrested were the government to open all its files on Amelia

Earhart, the problems which such a decision would entail must be recognized. The crucial issue is that of government responsibility. Can officials whose involvement in affairs of state leads them to desire that the truth about Earhart be kept confidential open their files and leave to the judgment of individual investigators the decision as to whether the truth should be publicized? Nevertheless, when branches of the government or military camouflage the truth by withholding information which is subsequently exposed, the public's attitude toward public statements grows more skeptical.

No matter which hypotheses or portions thereof eventually stand correct, the Amelia Earhart of 1937, admired and respected, "disappeared" that July 2, 1937. No one can bring back that singular person any more than the era of early aviation with all its daring trials and errors which led to eventual monumental accomplishments can be lived again except through memories, and when those have faded, through films and books. So long as the aura of mystery surrounds the "disappearance" of Amelia Earhart and Fred Noonan, the search will continue. However, might it not be contemplated that those who know the facts carry a far greater personal, social, and moral burden than those who seek the truth concerning Amelia Earhart?

BIBLIOGRAPHY

SOURCES FOR THE HYPOTHESES:

Briand, Paul, Jr. "Daughter of the Sky." New York: Duell, Sloan and Pearce, 1960.

Davidson, J. B. "Amelia Earhart Returns from Saipan." Canton, Ohio: Davidson, 1969.

Devine, Thomas E. Unpublished manuscript and correspondence.

Dwiggens, Don. "Hollywood Pilot." New York: Doubleday, 1967.

Goerner, Fred. "The Search for Amelia Earhart." New York: Doubleday, 1966.

Klaas, Joe. "Amelia Earhart Lives." New York: McGraw-Hill, 1970.

Morrissey, Muriel. "Courage Is the Price." Wichita: McCormick-Armstrong Publishing Division, 1963.

Nyberg, Bartell. The Search for Amelia Earhart. "Empire" (magazine section of the Denver Post) June 28, 1970. (Material on Robert Stanley)

Polhemus, William L. "Howland Island: ETA Thirty Years and Thirty Minutes." Burlington, Vermont: Polhemus Navigation Sciences, Inc., 1971.

SOURCES ON AMELIA EARHART:

Earhart, Amelia. "The Fun of It." New York: Harcourt, Brace, 1932.

BIBLIOGRAPHY

Earhart, Amelia. "Last Flight." (Arranged by George Palmer Putnam) New York: Harcourt, Brace, 1937.

Putnam, George Palmer. "Soaring Wings." New York: Harcourt, Brace, 1939.

SELECTED SOURCES ON JAPAN AND THE MICRONESIAN ISLANDS:

Borden, Charles A. "South Sea Islands." Philadelphia: Macrae Smith, 1961.

Clyde, Paul H. "Japan's Pacific Mandate." New York: Macmillan, 1935.

Gayn, Mark J. "The Fight for the Pacific." New York: William Morrow, 1941.

Grattan, C. Hartley. "The Southwest Pacific Since 1900." Ann Arbor: University of Michigan Press, 1963.

Hobbs, William H. "The Fortress Islands of the Pacific." Ann Arbor: J. W. Edwards, 1945.

Thomas, David. "The Battle of the Java Sea." New York: Stein and Day, 1969.

SOURCES ON THE ITASCA AND THE LEXINGTON:

Thompson, W. K. Excerpts from the Itasca Radio Log for June and July, 1937. Dated July 19, 1937.

Noyes, Leigh. Report of the Earhart Search: U.S.S. Lexington, July, 1937.

SELECTED SOURCES ON THE 1967 FLIGHT:

"Antique Airplane Association News." After 30 Years of Wandering the World TCA Comes Home. January-February, 1969.

Burke, John. "Winged Legend." New York: G. P. Putnam's Sons, 1970. (A biography of Amelia Earhart)

David, Diane. The 28,000-mile Mission of Ann Pellegreno, "Chicago Tribune Magazine," November 19, 1967.

Esch, Marvin L. Nation Honors Ann Pellegreno, "Congressional Record," July 12, 1967.

Hoorebeeck, Albert Van. "L'Histoire des tours du monde aeriens." Bruxelles, Belgium: Editions Wellprint, 1969.

Kohn, Leo J. Late-flowering Lockheed, "Air Progress," February 1968.

Pellegreno, Ann H. Around the World With EAA, "Sport Aviation," July 1968.

Pellegreno, Ann H. Destination—Howland Island, "Ninety-Nine News," October 1967.

Pellegreno, Ann H. Fly Around the World in a Thirty-year-old Lockheed? "Air Progress," June 1967.

Pellegreno, Ann H. I Completed Amelia Earhart's Flight, "McCall's," November 1967.

Pellegreno, Ann H. Lee and His Lockheed, "Air Progress," April 1968.

Pellegreno, Ann H. The Lockheed Comes Home, "Antique Airplane Association News," March-April 1968.

Ryan, John. "The Hot Land: Focus on New Guinea." New York: St. Martin's Press, 1969.

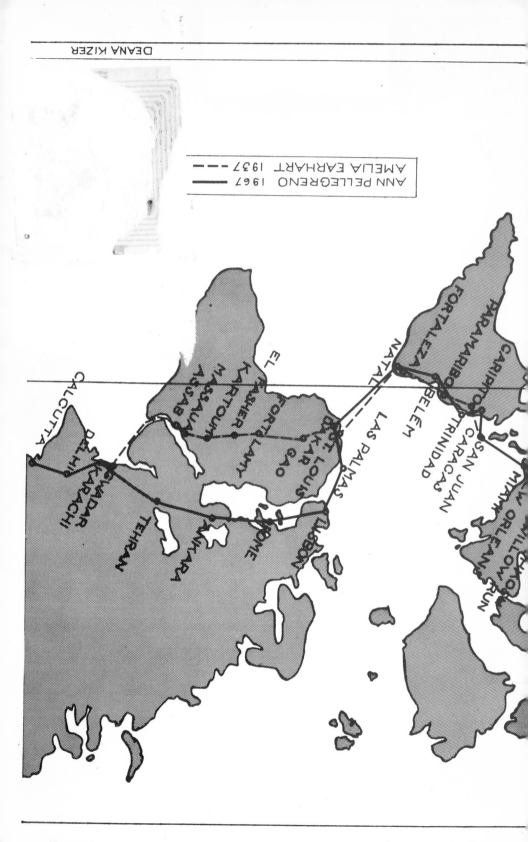

ANN PELLEGRENO 1967 ——
AMELIA EARHART 1937 ----